# KEY TO YOURSELF

*By*

DR. VENICE J. BLOODWORTH

DEVORSS *Publications*

ISBN: 0-87516-296-7

DeVorss & Company, Publisher
P.O. Box 550
Marina del Rey, CA 90294

Printed in the United States of America

# Key to Yourself

This book is for my Mother,
whose teachings are contained herein.
A very gallant and beautiful lady
whose dreams all came true.

# Contents

PROLOGUE . . . . . . . . . . . . . . . . . . . . .   7

I  THOUGHT, LAW . . . . . . . . . . . . . . . .   11

II  CONSCIOUSNESS, CONCENTRATION,
     THE SILENCE . . . . . . . . . . . . . . . . .   15

III  THE CONSCIOUS MIND . . . . . . . . . . .   19

IV  THE SUBCONSCIOUS MIND . . . . . . . . .   21

V  THE UNIVERSAL MIND . . . . . . . . . . .   25

VI  IDEAS AND AFFIRMATION . . . . . . . . . .   30

VII  SOWING THE SEED . . . . . . . . . . . . . .   35

VIII  FEAR . . . . . . . . . . . . . . . . . . . . . . . .   39

IX  MENTAL PICTURES AND
     IMAGINATION . . . . . . . . . . . . . . . . .   45

X  FAITH . . . . . . . . . . . . . . . . . . . . . . .   51

XI  SUCCESS . . . . . . . . . . . . . . . . . . . . . .   59

XII  ABUNDANCE . . . . . . . . . . . . . . . . . .   63

XIII  REALIZATION . . . . . . . . . . . . . . . . . .   70

| XIV | Health, Youth, Beauty | 76 |
| XV | Subconscious Impressions | 87 |
| XVI | Desire | 91 |
| XVII | Habit | 96 |
| XVIII | The Plenty Consciousness | 99 |
| XIX | The Law of Attraction | 100 |
| XX | Do Not Judge By Appearance | 102 |
| XXI | And the Greatest of These Is Love | 104 |
| XXII | Keying In | 105 |
| XXIII | Silence Is Golden | 106 |
| XXIV | It Is Never Too Late | 107 |
| XXV | More About the Subconscious Mind | 109 |
| XXVI | Disease | 111 |
| XXVII | The Food You Eat | 113 |
| XXVIII | Your True Self | 123 |
| XXIX | Prosperity | 124 |
| XXX | The Word of Power | 126 |
| XXXI | Happiness | 128 |

XXXII    THINKING IS THE REAL BUSINESS
           OF LIFE . . . . . . . . . . . . . . . . . . . . .   130

XXXIII    THE UNSEEN PATTERN . . . . . . . . . . .   132

XXXIV    CAUTION . . . . . . . . . . . . . . . . . . . . .   134

XXXV    TIME . . . . . . . . . . . . . . . . . . . . . . . .   135

XXXVI    DEPEND ON YOURSELF . . . . . . . . . . .   136

           SALUTATION TO THE DAWN . . . . . . .   141

           A BRIEF BIOGRAPHY . . . . . . . . . . . . .   143

           IN MEMORIAM . . . . . . . . . . . . . . . . .   149

# Prologue

*There was a door to which I found no Key;*
*There was a Veil past which I could not see;*
*Then to Heaven itself I cried,*
*"What Lamp has Destiny to Guide,*
*Her children struggling in the Dark."*
*"Understanding, Know Thyself!"*
*The wee small voice replied.*
                                        APOLOGIES TO OMAR

SINCE THE dawn of human existence and through all the succeeding ages mankind has recognized the mighty invisible force that governs and controls the universe and has tried to understand and use this power. In ancient China, in mysterious India, and beneath the shadow of the Sphinx, the seers and Prophets sought to lift the veil that shrouds the mysteries of life, and each race has made its quest for the Holy Grail. In every country on the globe we have found and are still finding the impress of each stage of bygone civilization, while history is a glorious record of man's upward climb toward truth and freedom.

The early savage awed by the phenomena of the sun, moon and stars, the mystery of life and death, found satisfaction by creating a primitive system of deities to whose supernatural powers he attributed those things beyond his own comprehension, and as we trace him down through the ages, we find his ideals gradually changing to fit his improved mentality, until today we stand on the pinnacle of those bygone centuries the intellectual giants of all ages.

We have reached the sublime heights in literature and art; science has revealed infinite resources and undreamed-of possibilities; invention has lightened the burden of harsh manual labor and given us comforts, conveniences, and educational facilities beyond the mental grasp of our ancestors while the future possibilities of electricity stagger the imagination.

Today more than ever before we find a tendency to question the meaning of life. By the efforts of the few we have reached the present stage of civilization, and because men are wiser today, they cannot be satisfied with anything less than the truth. THE TIME FOR INDIVIDUAL DEVELOPMENT HAS COME. WE MUST DISCOVER FOR OURSELVES THE WHYS AND WHEREFORES OF ALL THAT BAFFLES US IN THE MARVELOUS SCHEME OF LIFE AND NATURE. EACH OF US MUST FIND HIS OWN PLACE IN THE COSMIC ORDER, AND REALIZE FOR HIMSELF THE TRUE MEANING OF LIFE. INDIVIDUALLY WE MUST FIND THE KEY TO DESTINY.

Psychology is the answer. The science of mind is the science of life, for in mind all manifestation finds its common origin. All progress — whether individual, national, or racial — has been, and will continue to be, in the mental realm, and the greatest battle of the future will be one of ideas instead of guns.

The majority of people are drifting on the high seas of life. No chart marks their destination, no rudder holds a course. They are at the mercy of the

winds of chance, the rocks of doubt, the shoals of
ignorance, and if they make some progress before
the curtain falls, it is because they have used unconsciously the creative power, that is the birthright of every individual, and not any exact
knowledge.

In order that we may avoid aimless drifting,
with its wasted energy and its painful collisions,
we must know something of the mighty principles
that govern us and the world in which we live,
something of the great occult law of cause and
effect under whose operation our lives can be
filled with pain and poverty or joy and success.

In all the universe there can be no such things
as luck or fate; every action, every thought is governed by law. Behind every bit of good fortune lie
the causes that we ourselves have sometime,
somewhere set in motion. Behind all ill fortune
we will find the energy we, ourselves, have generated. Every cause must have a certain definite
effect, there is no dodging the results, we reap
what we sow with exact mathematical precision.

The writer has studied many religions and
philosophies, from those told in the flowery language of the mystic East to the crisp, clear, scientific findings of modern psychology, and in all we
find the same principles, the same immutable
laws, ageless, changeless, eternal, moving in silent
grandeur, laws that control our thought and from
which there is no escape, whether the law be put
into operation consciously or unconsciously.

It is apparent that a knowledge of these laws

and how to bring them into operation for the benefit of ourselves and others is the most practical
thing we could acquire, and in "The Key to Yourself" I have endeavored to set forth applied psychology in the simplest possible terms, so that
everyone regardless of educational advantages
may have an equal chance.

"The Key to Yourself" will take you into a
new world of accomplishment, prosperity, friends
and pleasure. It will give you a golden return if
you will study it correctly and steadily. The ines-
timable value of psychology cannot be compre-
hended by a mere reading or superficial knowledge;
its true worth can only be ascertained by study,
concentration and practice, and in all fairness to
the writer and yourself, you are requested to follow the methods set forth herein faithfully. If you
will do this, you will find that psychology will do
for you what it has done for others, that it will
actually produce the mental, physical, and material results for which you have so long been seeking.

THE AUTHOR

# I
# Thought, Law

*All is in the Silence waiting to be brought*
*Forth to form and substance by the builder, Thought,*
*That is how God fashioned everything He wrought,*
*Everything you long for, in the Silence wait,*
*Yours the power to shape them either soon or late,*
*But be very careful how you form your fate.*
—ELLA WHEELER WILCOX

THINKING is the true business of life. Thinkers rule the world. They always have and they always will. All people think, but the tragedy of life is that so few of us think creatively or constructively; so few recognize the fact that thought is a creative force. Every achievement in business, literature, philosophy, or science has found its source and expression through the mental efforts of the world's leaders. The outstanding figures of tomorrow are the creative and constructive thinkers of today.

We live in the same world and are as far apart as the difference in our thought processes. Some fail while others succeed; some are sick, others are healthy; some are miserable, others happy. We all want to blame luck or fate or some one of our fellow men, but the difference is within ourselves. We are the product of our prevailing habits of thought.

Each is building his own world from within; thought is the builder; subtle, vital, irresistible, omnipotent; and according as we use our thought forces do they bring us joy or sorrow, peace or pain, success or failure. Men, events and conditions are relative only; EVERY EXPERIENCE WITH WHICH YOU MEET HAS BEEN BUILT FOR YOU BY YOUR OWN INTERIOR THOUGHT PROCESSES.

The world without is merely a reflection of what you have acknowledged as true in your world within, so if the state of your health or finances is not all you desire, you must look within yourself for the cause. Regardless of what the condition is, or how it seemed to have come about, its cause had to find place in your consciousness before it came into expression. That a man can change himself, recreate himself, improve himself, control his environment, and master his own destiny is not a theory with the writer but a matter of positive knowledge.

There is no such thing as luck or chance; on the contrary our lives are governed by law, by actual, immutable principles that never vary. Law is in operation at all times, in all places; mighty, silent, fixed laws that underlie every human action, that bring to us, with exact precision, the full measure of our thoughts. Laws that favor no individual, and are no respector of persons. In a sense there is nothing in all the universe but law; every tree that grows, every flower that blooms, every snowflake that falls, testifies to the unceasing operation of this great law.

We all admit Natural Laws in regards to the

vegetable kingdom; we also accept the fact that the sun, moon, stars and tides of the sea are controlled by law, but it has not occurred to the majority of us that man is just as subject to law as the vast panorama of nature. It is law that makes the universe so harmoniously exact; if there was not law we could never be sure the sun would rise or the seasons come in rotation.

THERE IS BUT ONE LAW, ONE PRINCIPLE, ONE CAUSE, ONE SOURCE OF POWER. We cannot change the law, but by understanding and cooperation we may bring ourselves, through our thought processes, into harmony with the law and let the law work with us, through us, and for us.

It is natural for man to be healthy and whole in mind and body, and for him to abound in all good. When one learns this truth, and lives in accord with the laws of his being, health and prosperity spring forth naturally and abundantly.

The majority of people believe that peace and plenty on one hand, and poverty and sickness on the other is somehow interwoven in divine providence; but those who know the truth understand that life, health and abundance are a natural law of the universe, and thought is the active principle by which we are related to the things we need and desire.

THOUGHTS ARE THINGS. Thought causes vibration and sets in motion the Law of Mind. Since everything has its beginning in mind, and as thought, which is mind in action, produces form, we realize that thought is creative.

That which we call our subconscious mind, being a point in Universal Creative Law and being immediately available to us, guarantees that we have at our disposal the use of a law which is not only immediate, being inside of us, but it is also in connection with everything else in the universe.

It is the belief in separation from God which keeps our good away from us. It is the belief that binds us, and not any actual power. We are really bound by our false beliefs, and we shall never be permanently free until we experience a complete change of thought. This is what is meant by "The Renewing of the Mind."

# II
# Consciousness, Concentration, The Silence

*Our remedies in ourselves do lie*
*Which we ascribe to Heaven.*
—SHAKESPEARE

I SHOULD like for my readers to fully realize what consciousness means, for we may know something and it still not be a part of our consciousness. To illustrate: When you went to school and your teacher put the first example in long division on the board, she explained it as she worked out the problem and you saw it there, certainly you knew it could be done; no doubt entered your mind that long division was an accomplished fact, but you couldn't do it yourself until you had worked at it, studied it, concentrated on it for some time — then suddenly, perhaps, it came to you — you understood, you could "do" long division. That branch of mathematics was then a part of your consciousness. Do you see the difference? It is possible for us to intellectually perceive something without it being a part of our consciousness.

So it is with these lessons; just reading them will not do you any good, nor answer your purpose at all. You must study them, concentrate on them,

take them into the Silence with you until they
become a part of your consciousness.

There seems to be an idea that concentration
takes a lot of effort, but quite the reverse is true.
You know how we lose ourselves in an interesting
story until our surroundings are completely oblit-
erated — that is concentration — and we can so
train ourselves to meditation that we immerse our
minds in our subject to the exclusion of everything else. This power of attention is called the
Silence, and we should take a few minutes every
day to turn our thoughts within to take stock of
ourselves and to learn the truth.

You are not to expect any peculiar manifestation in the Silence; it is simply a physical stillness
where we shut out surroundings and sound, and
rest ourselves in mind and body, and learn to control and direct our thoughts into beneficial channels.

It would be well to gain control of the body
first, so for half an hour or so each day retire to
some place where you will not be disturbed, seat
yourself comfortably, relax every muscle and be
still. Let your thoughts roam over pleasant memo-
ries, but resolve to attain perfect control over your
body. Do not be anxious, but quietly understand
that we have plenty of time for everything and that
we are capable of doing everything we set out to
do. Practice makes perfect in all things. You may
not succeed the first few times, but persistent
efforts cannot fail to give you perfect physical
control. When you can do this you will find a new
poise and a new power pervading your entire

being, you will gain the first thrill of exultation that comes to those who conquer conditions.

The next step is to control your thoughts. Some people find it hard to think steadily on one subject for any length of time; our thoughts seem to want to jump from one thing to another, but we can select one subject, or object, and think on it, bringing our thoughts back every time they play truant, until we finally learn to think of anything we wish for ten minutes or more. Some people find these exercises hard, to some they are easy, but everyone can accomplish what they set out to do by patient effort.

It is absolutely necessary that you obtain self control both mentally and physically, because efficiency of any kind is contingent upon harmony, and there is no harmony where there exists a lack of control. When you learn self control you will be in position to think constructively and harmoniously; it is then you may "decree a thing and it will be established unto you." It is then you will understand with deeper reverence what the Master meant when He said, "Go into thine inner chamber and shut the door, pray to the Father in secret and He hearing in secret will reward you openly."

Thought is the only reality; conditions are but the outward manifestation of thought; as thought changes, all conditions must change in order to be in harmony with their creator, which is thought.

*This city with all its houses, palaces, steam engines, cathedrals and huge immeasurable traffic and tumult, what is it but Thought, but millions of Thoughts made into one — a huge immeasurable Spirit of Thought embodied in brick, in iron, in smoke, dust, palaces, parliaments, coaches, docks, and the rest of it! Not a brick was made but someone had to think of the making of that brick.*

—CARLYLE

# III
# The Conscious Mind

*If you think you are beaten, you are;*
*If you think you dare not, you don't;*
*If you'd like to win, but you think you can't,*
*It's almost a cinch you won't;*
*If you think you'll lose, you've lost,*
*For out in the world you'll find*
*Success begins with a fellow's will;*
*It's all in the state of mind.*

—SELECTED

E ACH INDIVIDUAL is endowed with two phases of mind, conscious and subconscious.

The conscious mind is that part of our mind with which we perceive, reason, judge, and reject; by its operations we are aware of our power to think, to know, to will, and to choose. Through the conscious mind we have conscious communication with every part of our body and respond to every sensation of sight, sound, smell, taste and feeling.

The conscious mind is the supreme ruler in our mental world; it deals with all impressions of the visible world, gathered through the five senses; it carries the responsibility of decisions and is the gateway through which our destiny comes. Through the Magic Portal of conscious, creative, constructive thought, wisdom, knowledge, and understanding bring their richest gifts and place the scepter of power in your hand; while health, wealth, happiness and youth trail their glittering robes across the threshold of your con-

19

sciousness and crystallize their royal attributes into your body and environment.

But if the thoughts entertained by the conscious mind are hate, envy, anxiety, weakness, fear, or other negative thoughts, then the Magic Portal becomes the Iron Door of despair through which poverty, disease and unhappiness drag their ragged garments into your life.

It is strange that we so long failed to understand the wonderful power of thought, for it is taught by every religion and philosophy in the history of the world. Paul, when in captivity and chained to a Roman soldier, gave to the world this message:

> Finally, brethren, whatsoever things are true, whatsoever things are honest, whatsoever things are just, whatsoever things are pure, whatsoever things are lovely, and of good report; if there be any virtue, and if there be any praise, think on these things.

Most of us have overlooked the meaning of that verse. We have been so busy admiring its beauty of diction that we failed to place emphasis on the word THINK. If everybody followed Paul's injunction and thought only in terms of truth, honesty, justice, purity and loveliness, this world would be transformed from a planet of confusion, sickness and poverty into one of radiant health, happiness and prosperity.

> *Earth's crammed with Heaven and every common bush is afire with God, But only he who sees takes off his shoes.*
>
> —E.B. BROWNING

# IV

# The Subconscious Mind

*The great were once as you.*
*They whom men magnify today*
*Once groped and blundered on life's way,*
*Were fearful of themselves, and thought*
*By magic was men's greatness wrought.*
*They feared to try what they could do;*
*Yet Fame hath crowned with her success*
*The selfsame gifts that you possess.*
*—EDGAR GUEST*

T HE SUBCONSCIOUS mind presides over all the involuntary processes of your body, such as digestion, assimilation, elimination, the beating of your heart, the circulation of your blood, the manufacture of various glandular secretions. It builds, sustains, repairs and operates the body. Under its direction new cells are born every minute.

So accustomed are we to these operations of the subconscious mind that for a long time science failed to recognize any distinction between our two phases of mind. Finally, however, positive proof of cell renewal directed by a central intelligence presented itself, and it was learned that while the subconscious mind faithfully and tirelessly keeps up its work of building and operating the body whether we are awake, asleep, or under the influence of an anaesthetic, it works under the control of the conscious mind.

The subconscious mind is the storehouse of memory, the seat of habit and instinct; it is also the center of emotion, and its action is automatic. The subconscious is that marvelous phase of your mind that brings things into existence by the sheer power of thought. It is the spiritual part of us and through it we are connected with the Divine and brought into relation with Infinite constructive forces of the universe.

The subconscious mind not only possesses the power and knowledge to build and repair your body; it is a part of the Universal Mind and has Infinite resources at its command. Dr. Jung tells us that the subconscious mind not only contains all the classified data gathered during all the past life of the individual, but that it contains also all the wisdom of all the immeasurable ages past, and that by drawing upon its wisdom and power the individual may possess the good things of life in great abundance. Dr. Jung also makes clear the fact that so long as the individual remains in ignorance of his subconscious power just so long does it remain a great unused force that can prove dangerous to our welfare. Ignorance of the existence and power of the subconscious mind is the cause of all the failures and near failures in the world.

On the other hand we can draw on the subconscious mind for all the wisdom and power necessary in the management of all our business and personal affairs. In fact, anything we leave absolutely to the subconscious mind to handle we will see accomplished.

The subconscious mind does not think, reason, balance, judge, or reject. It simply accepts all suggestions furnished by the conscious mind whether they be good or evil, constructive or destructive. Herein lies the mighty power of the conscious mind. The subconscious mind receives any idea or belief as a pattern to work by and proceeds to bring such ideas and beliefs into manifestation.

Prior to the development of our conscious reasoning power the subconscious mind works by a hereditary pattern, or race instinct. During childhood these subconscious activities are the result of heredity and environment demands and continue to be such unless we are fortunate enough to learn the unlimited power of our subconscious mind, though some people unconsciously draw on this power with most splendid results.

Thus we find the secret of good or bad results in child training is due to the fact that whatever training children get leaves its impression on the subconscious mind and makes the habits formed in our tender years the basis for all future actions unless we consciously and systematically set about to change them.

EVERY THOUGHT THAT ENTERS THE CONSCIOUS MIND IS SUBJECTED TO OUR REASONING POWER; IF WE ACCEPT AN IDEA OR THOUGHT AS TRUE, IT IS THEN CARRIED TO THE SUBCONSCIOUS MIND TO ACT ON AND IS BROUGHT FORTH INTO VISIBLE EXPRESSION AS A PART OF OUR PHYSICAL CONDITION AND IMMEDIATE SURROUNDINGS. THUS WE FIND THAT IN ITS LAST ANALYSIS

THE CONSCIOUS MIND DECIDES OUR FATE.
SO TO CONTROL OUR HEALTH AND ENVI-
RONMENT WE MUST CONTROL OUR
THOUGHT.

NOTE: Many writers speak of the "supercon-
scious mind" and refer to various grades of inner
perfection, but the term "subconscious" covers
all the unconscious part of us and is more easily
understood.

# V
# The Universal Mind

*Prate not of thy repentance, but believe*
*The spark divine dwells in thee; let it grow.*
*That which the upreaching spirit can achieve*
*The grand and all creative forces know;*
*They will assist and strengthen as the light*
*Lifts up the acorn to the oaktree's height.*
*Thou has but to resolve, and lo! God's whole*
*Great universe shall fortify thy soul.*

*—WILCOX*

THE UNIVERSAL mind is the source or common origin from which spring all manifestations.

If there is life there must of necessity be a source of life; if there is love there must be a source from which love comes. The same is true of wisdom, intelligence, health, happiness and what we call material things.

Charles Hanaal tells us in the "New Psychology" that:

> The Universal Mind is the substance of all force and form, the reality that underlies all existence. By it, in accord with fixed laws, all things are brought into being and sustained. It is the pure substance of Being, is everywhere present and is essentially the same at all points of its presence.

Herbert Spencer, the physical scientist, tells us the same thing when he says:

> Amid all the mysteries by which we are sur-
> rounded nothing is more certain than that we are
> ever in the presence of an Infinite and Eternal Energy
> from which all things proceed.

We are told by the Church on Biblical author-
ity that:

> In Him we live and move and have our being.

Since the dawn of human existence, and through
all the succeeding ages, mankind has recognized
the mighty invisible force that governs and controls the universe—that power by which and
through which all things are created. Some have
personalized this power and call it God, but the
most beautiful and the most comprehensive idea
of this power was given by Jesus when He talked
to the woman at the well. "God is Spirit." He did
not say "a" spirit nor "the" spirit, but simply
"God is Spirit," clearly indicating the presence of
God at all points at the same time. So we cannot
help but realize that the finding of the psycholo-
gist, the scientist, and the greatest of all Teachers
is one and the same. We must simply understand
the all important fact that there is but one principle, one power, one presence, and that this Omnipotent, Omniscient Presence is good.

Then we must realize that the subconscious
mind of the individual is one in kind and quality
with the Universal Mind, the only difference being
one of degree. We are individualized Spirit and
bear the same relation to the Universal Mind that

the sunbeam does to the sun. "Know ye not that ye are the temple of the living God." Here, then, is the secret of the wonderful creative power of thought. Thought is a spiritual activity; the only power which the spirit possesses is the power to think. Spirit is creative; therefore, thought is creative.

You know that the spirit of you is — you; that without the spirit you would be nothing. You also know that your thinking processes are directed by your spriritual power — but you have not considered the importance of this fact nor recognized its connection with the creative principles of the Universal Spirit of mind.

If you will stop to consider what the real "I" of you is, you will be astonished to find that it is neither your body nor your conscious mind. On the contrary, you will find that your mind and body are simply instruments used by the "I" of you to carry out its wishes. The "I" of you controls and directs both your mind and body and decides what they shall do and how they shall act.

The real "I" of you is eternal and is one with the Universal Mind. If you take a cup of water from the ocean, the water in the cup is still ocean water; there is just not so much of it and its power is not so great. Such is our comparison with the Universal Mind.

When you fully realize the true nature of this "I," you can never think badly of yourself again. Let your habits, characteristics, temperament be what they will, they compose your personality,

are subject to change, and have nothing to do with
the real indwelling self. The real "I" of you is
your subconscious mind and has the power to
change your physical condition and environment
through its connection with the Universal Mind.

Thought is the connecting link between us
and the Universal Mind, and considering this
marvelous fact, we arrive at the conclusion that
we ourselves are channels through which the Universal Mind pours itself into expression, and that
thoughts are causes and conditions are effects.

Thought being the cause, we cannot help realizing that if we control our thoughts, we control
effects; then it follows that our health, happiness,
and prosperity are under our control also. When
you understand this glorious truth, and realize the
wondrous possibilities open to you through your
connection with Omnipotence you will have found
"the Kingdom of Heaven within you."

We are so constituted that we fail to compre-
hend an entirely new idea. The conscious mind
must reach understanding through the vibratory
action of thought, and it is necessary for us to
study with undivided attention anything we desire
to learn. Your thought forces will lead you to the
realization of your fondest dreams, but make no
mistake in thinking these lessons are the royal
road to so-called miracles.

Psychology is the royal road to undreamed happiness, freedom and success, but you must pay the
price of concentration and study or this "Golden
Key" is not for you. All possession is based on

consciousness and you must establish a consciousness through understanding. A transfer of material things can be made, but wisdom must be bought by our own efforts.

We have the freedom of choice to express ourselves any way we see fit, and it is our duty to ourselves and our fellow men to express ourselves harmoniously and constructively. Sorrow, sickness, and poverty are quite unnecessary and are the results of ignorance of the truth. If you are manifesting any undesirable condition, change your ideas and viewpoint of life and a new set of conditions will appear.

"Spiritual things are spiritually discerned." We can get no understanding from the world of visible things; the things we see have no originating power in themselves. The world without is relative only; Truth is absolute and must be found by each individual within his own soul. Go into the Silence every day and concentrate on the fact that you are a spiritual being, a child of God and co-heir with Christ. Put aside every other thought except a desire for the truth. Ask for wisdom, knowledge and understanding as Solomon did and you will find as he did, that all else follows in their train.

> *Increase in me that wisdom that discovers my truest interest, Strengthen my resolution to perform that which wisdom dictates.*
> —FRANKLIN

# VI

# Ideas and Affirmation

*All the good the past has had*
*Remains to make our own time glad.*

THE UNIVERSAL Mind is Life, Love, Wisdom, Power, Health and Abundance in abstract perfection; man is the instrument through which these attributes are made concrete; and the VISIBLE EXPRESSIONS OF GOD'S PERFECT MATERIAL APPEARS IN THE FORM OF THE INDIVIDUAL IDEA THAT CALLS IT INTO BEING. The finest musician on earth could not do justice to his ability on an instrument that was out of tune. So with us, to get good results we must be in tune with the Infinite Mind.

To be in tune with the Universal Mind we must recognize the fact that mind is reality, and that ideas are the generating energy back of all existence; original ideas are not the products of the conscious mind but are furnished us by our subconscious mind and are spiritual. EVERYTHING IS FIRST AN IDEA. Every stage of human progress from the first stone hatchet of the cave man to the latest model flying machine of the present day was first an idea.

Everything is first worked out in the unseen ideal realm before it appears in tangible form. The realm of the unseen is the realm of cause; the realm of the seen is the realm of the effect. Paul, in the picturesque language of his day, stated this truth when he said:

*"So that which is seen hath not been made out of things which appear."*

This is the greatest discovery of all the ages, that ideas stand as cause to all that appears and that man can control ideas. This truth runs like a golden thread through all the religions and philosophies of the world's history; it has been told in parable, song and story by the seers and prophets of all ages. The beautiful story of Aladdin and his wonderful lamp was based on the fact that each individual possesses the indwelling power to condition his or her life in exact accord with what they would have it to be.

You remember that Aladdin only had to rub the lamp and a powerful genie appeared, ready to do his bidding. Fortune, fame, power, and the hand of a beautiful princess were his for the asking.

The lamp represents the conscious mind, the rubbing of the lamp means understanding, the genie represents the subconscious mind, that mighty power within yourself waiting for recognition and unfoldment, that when aroused and used will bring you to the realization of your fondest dreams. No matter what those dreams may be, their fulfillment lies in the Universal Mind ready to come into expression at your demand.

When you learn that you have the power to change everything about you, including your body, by changing your thoughts and ideas you will cease to worry over appearance of any kind, but will calmly set about changing your state of mind by using your imagination to establish a new set of ideas.

The best and quickest way to bring about reform in our thinking is by the use of a strong affirmation, to be repeated in the Silence and any time the need arises. The following: "I am healthy, strong, young, powerful, loving, harmonious, successful, and happy" is constructive and may be used with good results.

Your present character is made up of countless thoughts, beliefs, habits, entertained and formed by you in the past. This character is expressed on your subconscious mind and is the cause of your present health, your present state of mind, and your present financial status. If you wish to change all or any one of them the affirmation just given will be effective. This is true because any statement continuously made by the conscious mind is accepted by the subconscious mind as a pattern by which to weave your future. Your present conditions are the results of your past thinking. You will be what you are thinking today.

Some time ago in a speech the Governor of Pennsylvania said that he had been asked to give his opinion of what conditions would be in the United States twenty-five years hence. His reply was: "If I knew the predominant national thought of today, I could tell you what twenty-five years would bring forth." As with nations so with individuals. Whatever your predominant thoughts are, will be expressed in your health and surroundings, which means that your future is entirely under your own control.

It does not matter what your present condition may be, it rests with you to change it and make your future exactly what you would have it to be. There is no limit to the creative power of the Universal Mind and it is no respecter of persons, but moves in ageless, changeless, eternal silence bringing to you with exact precision the full measure of your thoughts.

You may ignore your subconscious and through this inner self your connection with the Universal Mind, but it is and will continue to be the basis of your existence. The all pervading intelligence behind the vast panorama of Nature, the intelligence that evolves every form of plant and animal life, that is all-wise and all-powerful, IS YOUR LIFE.

Man is the highest expression of individual life, because he thinks. We sometimes blame God for our misfortune, but the fact remains that we are entirely responsible for our success or failure, happiness or misery. Man makes himself, creates his own personality, character and circumstances.

Destiny is fixed by subconscious action; you are not the slave of circumstance, but the creator of your own destiny. We attract to ourselves only that which corresponds to our subconscious impressions, and you can always make a new start and create new conditions by changing your subconscious impressions.

If you have thought failure, think success; replace sick thoughts with thoughts of health. If there is any reason for unhappiness, resolutely put it out of your mind, for LIKE ATTRACTS LIKE, and the more you think of discordant conditions, the more such conditions will manifest for you. CONCENTRATE ON WHAT YOU WANT. When you do think you are impressing that desire on your subconscious mind; NEVER let your thoughts dwell on what you DO NOT WANT.

# VII
# Sowing the Seed

*Out of the past the present eternally springs,*
*You may sow what you will but tomorrow will bring*
*You the harvest to show you the manner of things*
*Is the seed you have chosen to sow.*
                                        —NEW PSYCHOLOGY

W E HAVE learned so far that thought is creative; that while we may think what we
choose, our thoughts are governed by immutable
laws; that the Universal Mind or Energy is the
basic fact of all existence; that there is but one
power or principle, pervading the entire universe,
and that through our subconscious mind, which
is a part of the Universal Mind, we may condition
our life in exact accord with what we would have
it to be. Now we will find out how we obtain good
results through our thinking processes.

When you want to raise cabbage in your garden
you PLANT cabbage seed; if you want beans or
corn you plant these respective seeds and you are
very careful to select seeds of the best quality.
You plant these different seeds in the same soil,
but you know that the perfection of your harvest
depends on the quality of your seed and your
careful attention during their growth; you are
never in doubt as to the nature of your product
because you know that where you PLANTED
corn, you will GATHER corn, and where you
PLANTED beans, you will HARVEST beans. WE

SOW AND GROW AND REAP OUR THOUGHTS
IN EXACTLY THE SAME WAY.

We reap what we sow, in kind and quality
with exact precision. The Law of Compensation
will not allow us to sow thoughts of one kind and
reap the fruits of another. We can be absolutely
certain that we will express outwardly the results
of our predominant thoughts.

Everything and everybody is governed by the
same law, and we should not expect to reap riches
from poverty thoughts; happiness from miserable
thoughts; health from disease thoughts; or peace
from angry thoughts; any more than we would
expect to gather tomatoes from gourd vines.

We sow our thoughts in our subconscious
mind and the law of growth brings them into
visible expression. If our thoughts are positive in
faith, desire, courage, determination, cheerfulness
and love, our physical condition and environment
will express these qualities in health, happiness
and prosperity. But if our thoughts are fear, hatred,
envy, anxiety, grief or jealousy, we will reap these
results in poverty, disease and misery.

Every time you think, you start a chain of
causation that will create a condition in strict
accord with the quality of thought which origi-
nated it. Whether we have success or failure, it
comes by the operation of exactly the same principle; the principle is unchangeable; its operation
is exact; we use the same principle and the same
substance to bring either good or bad results. IT IS

THE SEED YOU SOW THAT DECIDES THE
NATURE OF YOUR PRODUCT.

Let us use another illustration: Imagine everybody as being a miniature manufacturing plant,
our raw material is the limitless, inexhaustible
substance of Being; some of us turn out beautiful
homes, automobiles, fine raiment, health, happiness and everything else our hearts desire; others
work harder, are not so healthy, and gain a mere
competence; still others manufacture for themselves  poverty, disease and crime — yet we all
use the same substance or material; neither are we
restricted as to quality, the supply IS ALWAYS
equal to the demand — but we MUST make the
demand and supply the kind and quality of the
seed or idea.

Thus if a so-called sinner sows seeds of love
and faith, and a so-called saint sows seeds of fear
and bigotry, we should not blame God because the
sinner harvests peace and plenty and the saint
reaps bitterness. The Divine Mind knows neither
denomination nor creed, but works for all men
impartially and in justice and love.

God's universe is a universe of law and order
from its smallest expression to the circuit of the
solar system. GOD IS LAW. Man neither makes
nor breaks the law; he works with it or against it
as he chooses. and he reaps the pleasant or unpleasant results of his own decision. THERE IS NO-
THING EITHER MYSTERIOUS OR RELIGIOUS
ABOUT IT — IT IS SIMPLY THE LAW.

Let us remember that Universal Mind, Eternal Energy, Substance of Being, and Universal Life Principle all have the same meaning. However, the terms used will not matter when we understand that they mean God as the Divine Principle which rules the universe. The word "Principle" comes from the Latin word meaning "beginning," "fundamental truth."

# VIII
# FEAR

*What is the thought that is in your mind?*
*Is fear ever running through it?*
*If so, just tackle the next you find*
*By thinking you're going to do it.*
                                    —EDGAR GUEST

G OD CREATED us, but we make ourselves.
We are the architects and builders of our
own destiny. Our lives contain no joy that was not
born in our imagination, and crystallized into outward expression by the power of our own thoughts.
Sorrow, sickness and failure spring from fear, and
negative thinking, and are self-imposed — always.

We fear poverty, sickness, hard-luck, accidents
and disaster. We all have our own special brand of
fear, and what foundation have these fear thoughts?
NONE! They come from false appearance, heredity,
environment, race consciousness, and not one is
born of right thinking. They are the appearance of
evil. How are these negative thoughts to be overcome? Not by opposition, for opposition to evil
implies its reality, and evil of itself never was and
never can be real. We count as evil that which
does not bring good results, and the word "sin"
is attached to those acts which bring discord and
unhappiness. Evil and sin are not causes, but results; and cannot be placed among principles.

ALL PRINCIPLES ARE GOOD. IT IS ONLY
WHEN WE FAIL TO USE PRINCIPLES COR-

RECTLY THAT WE SIN OR FALL SHORT. "FAL-
LEN SHORT" IS THE ORIGINAL MEANING OF
THE GREEK WORD FROM WHICH OUR WORD
"SIN" IS DERIVED.

Our difficulties are due to ignorance of the
truth; we have accepted any sort of doctrine or
creed without very much consideration, but because the world has been taught for so long to think
that some must be rich, and some poor, that trials
and tribulations are a sort of predestined lot, that
this world is necessarily a vale of tears — is no
reason for us to keep on accepting any such ridicu-
lous creeds.

Look at Nature. How profoundly abundant she
is in everything. Can you suppose that the Mind
that imaged such profusion as we see on every
hand, ever intended you to be limited or to have
to scrimp and save and count pennies? No! You
don't believe it; after you stop to think it over you
must realize there has been a mistake somewhere.
We just have not understood that everything is
first an IDEA. So let us reform our ideas. All re-
forms must begin at cause. Cause is mind, and
mind does all its creative work in the Silence. Eli-
jah found God, not in the whirlwind, the earth-
quake, nor the fire, but in the still small voice.
Let us follow Paul's advice, "Be ye transformed
by the renewal of your mind."

Fear makes cowards of us; it makes us do
things we should not do and keeps us afraid to do
things we should. It is like the "Old Man of the
Sea" on our backs; it goes to sleep with us and
kicks us awake in the morning.

Whenever you find anything bothering you, start some sort of affirmation and hang on to it; do not give worry a chance; resolutely refuse to entertain any kind of negative thought. "The Lord is my Shepherd, I shall not want" helped me to get rid of financial worry and "There shall no evil befall thee, and neither shall any plague come nigh thy tent" was also comforting; read the 91st Psalm as many times as you can — you could not read it too many times — for in it you find a promise of deliverance from every evil, and even the fears of evil things. When you retire at night always repeat the affirmation, "I am healthy, strong, young, powerful, loving, harmonious, successful and happy."

When you repeat this affirmation, you are impressing your subconscious mind with just those qualities as a basis for the new character you are building, and this character will attract to itself conditions that correspond to it in kind and quality; you remember that the subconscious mind does not argue or prove, but goes to work and brings about conditions that the conscious mind believes to be true. "If you believe it, it is so," and if you fear any condition, fear being a very strong thought, you will be able to say with Job: "The thing I feared has come upon me." If a man is in debt he generally concentrates upon it, and not only ties the debt closer to himself but attracts more debt. Thus we use the Creative Principle constructively or destructively. Think about and concentrate upon what you want, NOT on what you do not want; substitute new constructive

ideas in place of those old worn-out beliefs; take
the load of worry, criticism, hopelessness off your
subconscious mind and let your light shine. It is a
poor rule that will not work both ways, and if you
have not been successful, healthy and happy in
the past — just let that dead past bury its dead —
turn your face to the sunrise of truth and forge
ahead. Nothing can stop you. Thoughts are causes
and conditions are effects; change the conditions
to suit yourself, and then you no longer have any
cause for fear or worry. There is only one principle, and that principle is good — "God is good
and good is all —"; therefore good only can have
reality or power.

It does not matter how many poor people you
see, or how many crippled or sick or unhappy
people there are in the world; that does not alter
the fact that the One Principle is good, and, when
used intelligently, will destroy every manner of
lack, limitation or disease exactly as light destroys
darkness. Turn on the light and there is no darkness; turn on the good and every seeming evil
disappears. "Judge not according to appearances—";
train yourself to realize that every form of discord
is but a mistake that should be simply corrected
in the same way that we would correct a sum in
addition. When we get the wrong answer to a
mathematical problem we have merely deviated
from the principle of mathematics; and we work
the problem over again; just so with life; when
things go wrong we have deviated from the Universal Life Principle and need only to correct our

thoughts to get into harmony again. So whenever you let your mind rest on any inharmonious condition you must realize that such conditions are apparent only. We hear a good deal about passing laws to correct this or that evil, but before any progress is made or any change is really effected the people must change their minds.

We are creatures of habit in both mind and body, so when we start in to change habits of thought we must be ever on our guard for when we seek to change ourselves in any way it seems as though everything goes against us. But, remember, that if we want to change our course when driving an automobile, we must stop, back, go forward and maybe back again before we get turned around; so in changing the impressions and habits of our subconscious mind we must experience some difficulty.

When the old poverty or distress thoughts try to argue with you just club them out with affirmations. Have a mental house cleaning and have one every day; remember that whenever you affirm that you are healthy and happy and prosperous, you are stating the exact truth and in perfect accord with the will of God for you. "Be ye perfect even as your Father in Heaven is perfect" is what Jesus knew to be the truth for every one of us.

When this truth becomes a part of your consciousness you will understand that you have nothing to fear.

Fear, anger, criticism and all such thoughts are the most expensive guests we can entertain. They bring a harvest of poverty, misery and discord. There is no need to fear anything for we carry the indwelling power to overcome everything. Then why should we be angry with our brother? If he has injured you, he will surely reap with interest everything he has done to you, and if you are angry in return you harm yourself more than him; and remember that the same mighty power that dwells in you, sleeps also in your brother. We are all children of the Father and co-heirs with Christ; so lift yourself above the petty manifestations of mistakes and live in accord with the good within you.

> One ship drives east, another drives west,
>    With the self-same winds that blow.
> 'Tis the set of the sails and not the gales
>    Which tells us the way to go.
> Like the waves of the sea are the ways of fate,
>    As we voyage along through life.
> 'Tis the set of the soul which decides the goal,
>    And not the calm or the strife.
>                            —ELLA WHEELER WILCOX

# IX

# Mental Pictures and Imagination

*The power is ours to make or mar*
*Our fate as on the earliest morn,*
*The Darkness and the Radiance are*
*Creatures within the spirit born*
*Yet, bathed in gloom too long, we might*
*Forget how we imagined light.*

—COLTON

E VERTHING is first worked out in the unseen, before it is visible in the seen; in the ideal before it shows forth in the real; in the spiritual before it manifests in the material. Your subconscious mind is bringing you the matured fruits of your mental action, so let's get busy and build something worthy of the latent powers within you.

Your imagination is a divine gift, for with mental images you may build any condition you desire. First comes the idea, then a mental picture of that idea; these are the thought seeds that the subconscious mind uses to grow our conditions and environment.

All possessions depend on consciousness. Do you want a home? Then build it in your imagination. It must be in your mind before it will ever be anywhere else. Don't stop to count the cost. You are not limited as to material; you are drawing on the inexhaustible Universal Supply. Build your house, fill in the details, furnish it after your heart's desire.

Every time a thought of lack tries to tell you, you are a fool, say to yourself: "I am rich beyond my fondest dreams. I have all the limitless substance of God to build with. There is nothing that my mind can conceive of, that I cannot have." And right there just remember that you built any undesirable condition that is manifesting in the same way, and by the same principle that you are building that home.

Of course, you did not consciously ask for poor health or financial embarrassment or anything else that you do not want, but not knowing the importance of controlling your thoughts, you went along with no definite end in view, no goal, blown along by Dick, Tom, and Harry's opinions; letting your mind sop up any opinion or statement without asking yourself whether such opinions were based on real facts or not, until you find yourself with a lot of beliefs, impressions, and opinions that have no foundation whatsoever.

Now if the Law works to bring about undesirable conditions on the hit or miss plan that most people use, it will certainly work better to produce conditions that are systematically thought out and concentrated upon with a definite end in view. In fact, it will work much better to bring good conditions, because good is in accord with principle, and every time the beautiful, joyous possibilities of realizing your ambitions seem too good to be true just get the fact that mind or thought is the ONLY CREATOR; that thinking is real, the true business of life; and that your results will be in exact accord, both in kind and quality, with your thoughts.

DO NOT THINK THAT YOUR SUPPLY OR YOUR WAYS AND MEANS MUST COME TO YOU THROUGH ANY SPECIAL CHANNEL. TO DO THIS IS TO LIMIT YOUR AVENUES OF SUPPLY. THE UNIVERSAL MIND CAN BE DEPENDED UPON TO OPEN THE WAY BEFORE YOU TO BRING ABOUT YOUR DESIRE.

You cannot teach the Creator. The power that thought the universe into expression does not need to be advised by you. "Ask and you shall receive." You must, however, supply the idea or mental picture, and you must make the image clear, and hold it, concentrate on it until it becomes the only real thing to you. Want it with all your mind and heart and strength. Expect what you want and nothing else. Give no thought to external conditions, build your IDEAL in the world within and the Law of Attraction will certainly and surely bring it to you.

The law is that "like attracts like." Whatever you hold in mind for any length of time MUST come into expression for you. No matter what it is you desire—health, business, a new job, automobile, home or anything else—just make a clear mental picture of it and hold it in mind as your own; the way will be opened for you and you will have the joy of knowing you can be what you will to be, and no restriction can be placed on you, for your subconscious mind has no pattern with which to mold your future except that furnished by your conscious mind.

Everything that has ever been accomplished has been done by visualization. Every building was first in the architect's mind; every picture painted was the brain child of an artist; every invention was first an idea in the inventor's mind. The law of cause and effect is absolute and undeviating. Thought precedes and determines every action and manifestation, so when we fix any goal, and concentrate on that purpose we may be sure of our results.

That is the law and it always has been the law, and is still the law. Even if you should try to do something and seem to fail, try again and keep on trying. If a building or bridge falls we do not think the law of gravity has failed. We know the building or bridge was not strong enough. A hundred years ago we had as much electricity as we have now, but it did not do us any good until someone found the law by which to make it serve us.

It will prove so with you when you have established the consciousness of your oneness with the Universal Mind and your power to use the Law. Your needs will not even reach the stage of needs. You will find the way prepared before you realize the desire. "Before they call I will answer them and while they are yet speaking I will hear."

You must have a goal for which you are willing to strive. Some people do not succeed because they just dwaddle along and watch the clock for quitting time. They reap what they sow — failure — others work well, but have no goal and no faith in themselves; they are timid and easily believe in calamity and consequently never get anywhere.

Decide what you want and stick to it. If you were cutting a figure from a block of stone and changed your model every few days, all your efforts would be useless. You would cut your stone away and have nothing to show for your efforts. So it is with building our future. When you sow seed thoughts for some special purpose, hold it in mind until you have acquired your desire in objective form. You cannot fail if you want anything hard enough to make the proper mental effort to impress your desire on your subconscious mind.

It has been commonly supposed that the dreamer is a failure, but he who builds his future in his imagination with faith and purpose, never fails to realize his desire. Of course, merely wishing for anything or just to let your fancy run riot is wasted effort, because when you wish you do not believe you can obtain your wishes and you are really saying to your inner power, "I certainly would like to have so and so, but it is beyond my means." To use your mental powers in this way is to sow failure.

Be positive, do not say, "I'd like to have," but, "It is MINE." Whenever you claim anything by faith never go behind that statement. Let every effort of yours be mentally listed as carrying you nearer your goal. When Jesus said, "As thy faith is, so be it unto you," He made a statement that is today considered a SCIENTIFIC FACT.

There are times when even the bravest want to give up; times when appearances indicate that everything is against us, and it is no use to try. At such times you should remember that it is always darkest just before the dawn; that a little more faith, a little more patience is all that we need to win. Remember, too, that all those who have reached their goal ahead of you felt tired sometimes, and wanted to give up, but they DID NOT. If they had, you would never have heard of them.

Occasionally we are like the little boy who went off to find the "Wishing Gate." He was so intent on his purpose that he did not notice where he was going. Presently he found that he was lost and very tired, so he sat down on an old stile to rest. The North Wind came along and offered to take him home, and he abandoned his quest because he was tired and accepted the North Wind's offer.

As they traveled along the North Wind asked him how he came to be lost. "I was looking for the Wishing Gate," he replied. The Wind laughed all the way to his home. When they reached his doorstep the North Wind said, "The next time you go out to search for anything keep your wits about you. You were sitting on the Wishing Gate when I found you."

# X
# Faith

*All are but parts of one stupendous whole,*
*Whose body Nature is and God the Soul.*

—POE

I F WE would only understand that God is not
some far-off Deity; not a stern Judge, but the
beneficent force that we recognize as Nature—the
Life Principle that makes the flowers bloom, and
the plants grow; that spreads abundance about us
so lavishly.

If we could realize that there is no lack, want,
limit, or restriction in the Universal Mind. The
supply is limitless, inexhaustible and free-flowing
to all God's children and creatures. "Prove me
now herewith, saith Jehovah of Host, if I will not
open the windows of Heaven and pour out such
blessings that there shall not be room to receive
it." The blessings are piled mountain high for you
but you must have the faith to "Prove me now
herewith."

Paul tells us that: "Faith is the substance of a
thing hoped for, the evidence of a thing unseen."
Give that a moment's thought — Faith is the
SUBSTANCE, the actual substance of anything
we desire. The reason we have not demonstrated
more faith is because of our lack of understanding.
We have not understood that everything works in
exact accord with a definite law. We must build
our desires in our world within, build them in

51

faith, hope, courage, and hold them regardless of outside appearance. Pay no attention to appearance. Your success, your happiness and your health are all of your own making, and if you are not satisfied with conditions as they are you have only to visualize them as you would have them to be in order to change them.

The Law will work for you every time when you are working with the Law and for the good of all concerned; whether for health, success, sunshine, shower, or whatever it is — you can so protect yourself, your home, your business, that nothing in the universe can harm you.

When Christ told Peter to come to Him walking on the waves, Peter looked at the water and began to sink. His faith was weakened by looking at the dangerous appearance of the waves. Jesus REPROVED PETER FOR JUDGING BY APPEARANCE. He did not reprove anything outside of Peter, though the waves were rough. He did not say to Peter, "If these waves are smooth, or if there was a bridge here you could come," BUT REGARDLESS OF THE EXISTING CONDITIONS He had said, "Come!" And He reproved Peter for lacking something he should have had within himself. "O thou of little faith, wherefore didst thou doubt."

Because the power of the Universal Mind is invisible is no reason to doubt it. All the generating powers of existence are invisible; we cannot see Life except as a motive power; love is invisible, yet no one doubts love; and we only see the effects of happiness, peace and health. The same Law that works for us is the Law that Christ used and gave to His disciples. It is just as available to us today as it was when God said, "Let there be Light." The Universal Supply is all around us, and it forms in us and about us according to our thoughts.

When the first World War began the Germans took for their slogan: "Christmas dinner in Paris!" But when the great crisis came and the Germans were almost triumphant, the French people, even the women and children, took up the cry: "They shall not pass!" Instead of dining in Paris, the Germans retreated. An impassable barrier was built by the faith of the people of France. "Not by might, nor by power, but by my Spirit, saith Jehovah."

We read of the Oriental tribes observing a religious custom that requires its followers to walk barefoot over red hot coals. The fact that they do so without the least injury to themselves shows that these people possess the power of faith. It also proves that faith is an individual attainment dependent only on the power of the individual to believe, and is not confined to any race or creed. Those who visit the shrines of St. Roche in New Orleans, Guadalupe in Mexico, Lourdes in France, Ann Beaupre in Canada, are astonished to see the crutches and canes left at these places, silent reminders that faith does heal.

The law of faith is universal; it is just as powerful and just as available now as it ever has been, and every desire of our hearts is included in its rich promises to all men.

God never gave poverty to one man and riches to another, neither has He ever brought sickness to you and health to your neighbor; Life, health and abundance are omnipresent. The only law of nature is the LAW OF SUPPLY. Poverty is unnatural; it is distinctly a man-made condition, brought about by the limits man places upon himself. God's gifts are equally available to everyone. Health, Happiness, and Prosperity are not limited either to time, place or individual; they are a matter of consciousness and are attracted to those who understand and believe in their own inherent powers to achieve.

In the 11th chapter of Mark, the Nazarene gives us the key, not only to unlimited achievement, the law by which we may bring anything into manifestation, but shows also the fact that the Universal Mind works in accord with our demands regardless of whether the results be good or bad. He had cursed the fig tree the day before and Peter called his attention to the fact that the fig tree was dead. (This is the only record of Christ having used the creative principle destructively.)

Jesus answered Peter saying: "Have faith in God. Verily I say unto you, whosoever shall say unto this mountain, be thou taken up and cast into the sea; and shall not doubt in his heart, but shall believe that what he saith cometh to pass; he shall have it. Therefore I say unto you All things whatsoever ye pray and ask for, believe that ye receive them and ye shall have them."

Christ used the illustration of the mountain to impress on the minds of His followers the fact that ANYTHING is possible to those who believe, and the wording of both sentences indicates that our faith must be absolute to the extent that we believe our petition as already an accomplished fact. "All things whatsoever ye pray and ask for believe that ye receive them," or BELIEVE THAT YOU ALREADY HAVE THEM. This is the KEY to God's unsearchable riches. BELIEVE THAT YOUR DESIRE IS AN ALREADY ACCOMPLISHED FACT.

Make a mental image of what you pray and ask for, build it firmly in your imagination, claim it as yor own, close your eyes and SEE IT. Then realize that you have created your desire from the invisible substance all about you. BELIEVE THAT YOU HAVE IT, and you can safely leave ways and means for its material manifestation to the Universal Mind.

Let us reason together on that, "Believe that you already have it" idea. You have learned that the Law of Growth brings our wishes into being in the same manner that our garden seeds are brought to maturity. Now after you plant your seeds in the ground you cannot see them but you know you planted them, so you go ahead and cultivate your ground in FAITH. If you did not have a reasonable faith that your seed would grow vegetables you would not work them, but you do have faith and you proceed on the idea that your garden will produce so much garden truck at a given time. YOU ARE REALLY CONSIDERING YOUR GARDEN AS AN ALREADY ACCOMPLISHED FACT. Perhaps it has not occurred to you that you are doing that, but just think it over and you will realize that you do; and furthermore you think of EVERYTHING you accomplish in the same way.

Because the universal substance is invisible and thought is invisible we feel less confidence in the idea that our desires are accomplished before they come into visible expression, yet we must plant our thoughts and grow them exactly as we do a visible seed for that is the only way you have ever acquired anything. The fact that you sowed your seed unconsciously, and for that reason did not always get good results, does not alter the situation in the least.

Poverty, unhappiness and disease are the results of a belief in such conditions. These conditions are not only UNNECESSARY, but they are UN-NATURAL. There is no limit or restriction in the Universal Mind and you may have anything you want if you will demand it according to law. Make your mental picture clear and distinct. Take time every day to enter your mental world and live with your ideals awhile, realize that your present conditions were unconsciously made by the same process that you are now consciously using. Do each day what your hands find to do, learn to expect only that which is good, and expect only what you want. Have a mental house-cleaning every day, throw away every mental indication of lack or discord, and watch events shape themselves for your benefit.

Why did the Nazarene tell us that we must become as little children before we could enter the kingdom of Heaven? Simply because the faith of a little child is perfect. Everything you tell a child is accepted at its face value, for children have no adverse experience and fears to counteract their faith.

You remember the story of the crowd of people who congregated in church to pray for rain and no one brought an umbrella except one little girl. The rain came while they were praying and everybody got wet except the small lady whose faith really brought the rain, and the preacher who shared her umbrella.

It is the absolute, unquestioning faith that brings results. The faith of the little girl who prayed for rain was so absolute that she carried an umbrella. Such faith never fails because the thought is positive. The Kingdom of Heaven is within you, but to enter that kingdom you must wrap yourself in the mantle of a little child's faith. It is the mission of applied psychology to teach the truth of your relation to the Father, so that your faith may rest on the solid foundation of understanding.

Remember how rose colored everything used to be when we were children? How we used to roll on the grass and laugh just for the pure joy of being alive? Try to recapture some of the joy and faith of childhood. Strip your mind of worry and care, grab your faith with both hands and enter that Magic Kingdom where "eye hath not seen or ear heard, neither has it entered the hearts of men — the things God had prepared for those who love Him."

*Tradition whispers that in the sky is a bird,*
*blue as the sky itself, which brings to its finders*

*happiness. But everyone cannot see it; for mortal eyes are prone to be blinded by the glitter of wealth, fame, and position, and deceived by the mocking Will-o-Wisp of empty honors. But for the fortunate ones who seek with open eyes and hearts, with the artlessness, simplicity, and faith which are richest in childhood, there is an undying promise; and to them the Blue Bird lives and carols, a rejoicing symbol of Happiness and Contentment unto the end.*

—FROM THE NEW PSYCHOLOGY

# XI
# Success

*For the best verse hasn't been rhymed yet,*
*The best house hasn't been planned*
*The highest peak hasn't been climbed yet,*
*The mightiest rivers aren't spanned.*
*Don't worry and fret, faint hearted*
*The chances have just begun,*
*For the Best jobs haven't been started,*
*The Best work hasn't been done.*
                              —BRALEY

B EYOND the horizon of today are the problems of tomorrow; in your method of thinking lies either success or failure. What are you thinking? Where are you drifting and what is your harvest to be? Do you remember how joyously we used to spend our last dime for a magnet? Because we never wearied of watching the "horse shoe" pick up needles, nails and pieces of steel.

The magnet illustrates the Law of Attraction, and it is by this same principle that we draw to ourselves through positive and negative polarity those things, conditions, events and people to whom we are properly attuned. Life gives back to us exactly what we give. We externalize in the objective world what we store up in our world within. The law of expression is that we must ultimately express in objective form those thoughts, emotions and impulses which we have stored up in our subconscious mind.

The law of the subconscious mind is suggestion. The subconscious mind does not think, reason, balance, judge or reject. It simply accepts all suggestions furnished by the conscious mind; whether they be good or evil, constructive or destructive. Therefore the secret of success is to store your subconscious mind with desire, ambition, courage, determination, enthusiasm and faith in yourself. Add to these indispensable attributes love for your fellow man and faith in the ultimate good of all things.

Have faith in your inherent power to achieve; it is faith in yourself that attracts success. If you do not limit your capacities they will have no limit. The Universal Mind sees all, knows all and can do all. We share in this absolute power exactly to the extent of our faith, belief and purpose. Our mental attitude is the magnet that draws to us everything we need to bring our desires into being.

Find out how much your ideas are worth to you. You can image big things as easily as little ones; put your creative imagination to work. Start something! Imagine things, not as they are, but as you would have them. Create a place for yourself in your imagination and hold it steadily. If you want a certain position, claim it as your own and "SEE" yourself doing it. Do not let any lack of training, education, or any other kind of "BUTS" get in your way. Your subconscious mind knows more than all the book learning in the world can give you; education helps one to succeed, but

some of the greatest failures have been highly educated, while Andrew Carnegie, after he had made
millions, employed a tutor to teach him the essen-
tials of education.

Ben Franklin's future wife laughed at him the
day he landed in Philadelphia because of his ridi-
culous appearance, yet we pay tribute to Franklin
every time we turn on our electric lights.

Abraham Lincoln was born in a frontier cabin
minus a floor; reared in poverty and handicapped
by an awkward body. The mighty soul of Lincoln
surmounted every barrier, led him to the loftiest
heights and enshrined him for all time in the
hearts of his people.

And the Nazarene, whose pure white torch
lights the way for untold millions, the Savior,
who recast the drama of civilization, and whose
teachings we are just beginning to understand —
was born in a manger. With these mighty exam-
ples before us we cannot help but realize that
what a man is and does depends entirely on the
use he makes of his indwelling power.

This is the age of mind. Men are thinking
today as they never thought before. Invention has
lightened the burden of labor, science is proving
to us the truth of principle underlying every human
action, and the greatest discovery of all is the fact
that we can take our lives out of the hands of
chance, and place ourselves on the sure foundation of the law of cause and effect.

Right thinking plays the most important part

in our lives. Most of us merely reflect the opinions of others; we fear the search for truth; our occupation, politics, religions, and social relations are usually due to heredity or the pressure of environment.

The explorers, prophets and empire builders have all been men who dared to come out of the ruts, think new thoughts, and find new trails. Shake off the old worn-out prejudice, ignorance and superstitions. The world needs real thinkers for they are the men who led us out of the stone age.

*Cause and effect are as absolute and undeviating in the hidden realm of thought as in the world of visible and material things. Mind is the master weaver, both of the interior garment of character and the outer garment of circumstance.*

—ALLEN

# XII

# Abundance

*We build our fortune thought by thought,*
*For so the universe was wrought,*
*Thought is another name for fate:*
*Choose then the destiny and wait,*
*For love brings love and hate brings hate.*
                    —VAN DYKE.

W E CANNOT doubt the fact that abundance is a natural law; everywhere we look Nature is lavishly, wastefully extravagant; every seed that grows brings forth "fifty, a hundred and a thousand fold." Nowhere is economy displayed in any created thing.

There is abundance of health, happiness and prosperity for everyone and your supply does not depend on any living creature but yourself. The Law of Attraction operates unceasingly and brings to you your own regardless of existing circumstances. I know that sounds too good to be true, but let us prove it.

Among your friends is a man whom everybody considers a live wire; he is cheerful, hopeful, greets you with a million-dollar smile, makes a success of everything he touches, and you say: "That is one lucky guy." Now call to mind the party who is always complaining, nothing ever goes right with him or her; they are either sick or bankrupt or some one has swindled them, etc. Then there

are the very economical, narrow-minded ones
who find something to criticize everywhere they
go. Now just take stock of those people and see if
their health and environment does not correspond
exactly with their mental attitude.

WHEN YOU REALIZE THE FACT WE EX-
PRESS ABSOLUTELY IN BODY AND SUR-
ROUNDINGS WHAT WE THINK, YOU WILL
UNDERSTAND WHAT IS MEANT BY "GOD IS
A JUST GOD." AND "THINE OWN WORDS
SHALL BE THY BURDEN."

The difference in men is almost wholly due to
the difference in their thoughts. Therefore, you
can readily see that to have health you must concentrate on health; to be loved you must love your
brother; to have abundance of material wealth you
must think abundance. THAT IS THE LAW AND
NO PERMANENT GOOD WAS EVER ACQUIRED
IN ANY OTHER WAY.

If you lay a lot of steel shavings on a barrel,
every time some one jars the barrel some of the
shavings will fall off; but put a magnet under them
and you may turn the barrel upside down and the
shavings will stick. So it is with human beings;
WHATEVER YOU HAVE MADE YOURSELF A
MAGNET FOR, YOU WILL GET.

You have seen people work and strive for something and just when everything seemed coming
their way the unexpected element stepped in and
destroyed all their efforts. On the other hand, we
see people who gain everything they wish with
very little effort. Everything just seems to happen

for them. It is the appearance of such things that leads people to believe that fate or luck worked for some and against others. THE CAUSE FOR EVERY CONDITION BEING THOUGHT AND INVISIBLE IS NOT TAKEN INTO CONSIDERATION.

The effects, good or bad, may arise from any number of sources, but the CAUSE HAD TO ORIGINATE IN THE MIND OF THE INDIVIDUAL AFFECTED. This is so true that you may gauge a man's mental capacities by taking stock of his physical condition and his immediate environment.

The greatest barrier to individual progress is a slavish devotion to precedent. We do what everybody else does; we believe with the majority, without inquiring whether a doctrine is based on a myth or is a scientific fact. If these beliefs were transient mental impressions, no harm would be done, but when an idea sinks into the subconscious mind it comes forth as material results and while we do not realize it, we unconsciously fight any opposition to these submerged tendencies. That is the reason it is so hard to overcome a long established habit.

The only way to overcome error is to know the truth; to know that mind is the only creator and that we may consciously create any condition in body and affairs by holding a mental picture of the desired condition.

The fact that we build ourselves both in body and environment should not seem so strange when we consider that such an arrangement is the only way we could be absolutely free, and freedom was promised us by the Nazarene when we learned the truth.

Every man's ideas and desires are different; what is plenty for one would be poverty for another. The work one man finds pleasure in would bore another to extinction; but when we find that each may call into being his very own desires by going to the great storehouse of inexhaustible spiritual wealth, that we may be healthy, happy and prosperous by impressing our desires on our subconscious mind, we begin to understand something of the mighty power, wisdom and justice of the "Father." And it is so beautifully simple.

Suppose you had a great store of raw material that would produce anything according to individual desires and you have many children whom you wished to provide for, but desired that they reach their highest efficiency without restriction. You would say to them: "Here is unlimited material that will create good or evil conditons for you exactly as you call it into being. Take your choice and you must abide by your own decision."

That is exactly our relation to the Father, and the Christ understood this law perfectly when He said: "Whatsoever things ye desire when ye pray believe that ye receive them, and you shall have them." You will note the unrestricted "whatsoever things," meaning that no limit is placed on the individual. Divine Mind is as much present in the infinitely large as in the infinitely small and responds as readily to one demand as another.

In the verse following the one just quoted we are warned that to acquire "whatsoever things," we must, "when we stand praying, forgive if you have aught against any one; that your Father also — may forgive you." Thus we find that we may sow thoughts for our heart's desire, but to reap what we want we must be careful not to harbor anger, jealousy or criticism against any one. To do so is to fail altogether in realizing our desires or reap them mixed with unwelcome attributes.

There is a deep-rooted conviction in our minds generally that Christ taught the "beauty of poverty and self-denial." No greater error was ever made; and there is nothing in His teachings to support any such theory. On the contrary, He taught the fact that "all things are possible" to him who believes.

Jesus Christ was never ambiguous. He never used words or figures of speech for effect. He meant what He said, wholly, exactly what He said. His marvelous consciousness of oneness with the Father gave Him powers of concentrated expression that no other man has ever approached, and His every word and action showed an all-absorbing desire to give man health, happiness and abundance.

In His talks to the multitudes He pleaded with men to ask anything in His name. "Ask and you shall receive." "Hitherto you have asked nothing in My name, ask and you shall receive that your joy may be full." "All things whatsoever you shall ask in prayer, believing — you shall receive."

It was Christ's mission to teach the truth (the

spirit of the law) and He made every effort to establish truth by arousing man's faith in His own indwelling power and a realization of "the Kingdom of Heaven is within you."

Science has proved to us that every material thing is composed of the same substance, and that that substance is omnipresent; Christ proved His absolute knowledge of this law by materializing loaves and fishes out of the air; thus we are forced to realize that He knew there was no such thing as poverty, and when we consider His numerous healings we know that He understood that the only physical law was the law of health; then when He said: "Seek ye first the Kingdom of God and His righteousness and all these things shall be added unto you," He was simply telling us where to find the unfailing supply for every need including our material blessings.

Many people think that "seek ye His Kingdom" meant that Christ wanted us to kill our every desire for food, clothing, houses, land, recreation, amusement and seek only after an unknown God and His spiritual Kingdom. The Christ who wore the seamless robe, the most exclusive and expensive garment of His age; the Christ who changed water into wine to save His hosts embarrassment; who called loaves and fishes out of the air to feed the hungry; who raised the dead, restored sight, hearing and health to all who asked. The Christ whose every act in life contradicts such a belief.

So let us clear our subconscious mind of belief

in poverty, distress, sickness and seek the Kingdom of Heaven within us where "all these things"
are added unto us. Let us realize, as the Nazarene
did — "It is not I that doeth the work, but the
Father that dwelleth in Me doeth His work." Let
us recognize the fact that lack, limitation and disease exist only in the minds of those who fail to
perceive the truth — then recognize, realize and
use your birthright of life, health, happiness and
abundance.

*For My words are spirit and truth and life,
they shall not return unto Me void, but shall
accomplish that whereunto they are sent.*

# XIII
# Realization

*Ye shall know the Truth*
*And the Truth shall make you free.*

THIS IS the age of mind; the age of inquiry; the age of discovery; and the greatest discovery of all the ages is the discovery of thought force and the power of thought.

This great fact is as yet unknown to the majority of mankind. Too long have we been taught to look without for help, while the mighty power of our subconscious mind has been used ignorantly or not used at all while we struggle along on our surface power, which means that we are using about ten per cent of our mentality, for ninety per cent of our mental power is subconscious.

In using this ten per cent we deal with effects, looking always to the evidence of the five senses, while the marvelous powers and uses of Idealization, Visualization, Concentration and Realization are completely ignored.

Is it any wonder that we find sickness, poverty and misery on every hand when we ignore the cause and deal always with effects? The visible material things have no originating power within themselves. Everything we see is the result of an idea; and we must REALIZE this truth before we can rise above and free ourselves from any condition.

Environment of any description is the manifestation of ideas. If the conditions are unsatisfactory, build new conditions in your mind, ignore the present surroundings and hold fast to your mental picture. THE REALIZATION OF YOUR POWER TO DO THIS IS THE TRUTH THAT MAKES MEN FREE.

Can you, do you, realize the importance of this wonderful truth? You must realize your power before you can use it. Realization or consciousness of your potential ability to bring about any necessary change in your body or affairs is absolutely essential. Arouse, strengthen and believe in that wonderful inner self.

Knowledge is of priceless value. The astronomer who foretells the appearance of a comet is in nowise disturbed by the celestial visitor, but the ignorant savage is frightened by what he does not understand. The man who knows his own power to manifest his desire and control conditions remains calm and confident under any sort of circumstance, but the man who has no knowledge of his own power is at the mercy of every wind that blows. "With all thy getting — get understanding."

We use the invisible Spirit Substance to build ourselves physically and environmentally, and our results are in exact accord with what we ARE. We must give mentally before we can get; what we get depends on what we are, and what we are depends on what we think. A woman who understands bread making can take flour, milk, soda, salt, shortening, and make delicious biscuits, provided the ingredients are of GOOD QUALITY. So it is with the use of the Spirit Substance; we must first have knowledge of our power, and think thoughts of good quality; when we do this we build a perfect body and delightful conditions.

On the other hand, give the woman who cannot cook the finest ingredients that the market affords and she will turn out a bread a pup couldn't eat. Her intentions are good and she tried, but she did not KNOW how to cook and failed.

The same rule applies to all trades and professions. It is the master hand that creates anything worthy of the material used, and no first effort is a credit to the creator; but just as we grow skilled by using constant effort in any given line so we will gain confidence, faith and power by repeated efforts to realize and use our indwelling creative power; remember that no success is acquired in anything without CONCENTRATION.

Let no material evidence of the five senses stand in your way. Just because psychology is a new doctrine to the majority is no reason to disbelieve the truth. People loudly disclaimed the fact that the earth is round; when science discovered the sun in the center of the solar system with the earth spinning around it, everybody knew it could not be so simply because they had been taught that the earth was flat, that the sun rose every morning and set every evening, and did not every one SEE the sun travel across the heavens and set behind the western hills? Yet today no one doubts that the earth is round, that it travels around the sun every year and turns completely around every twenty-four hours.

So it is evident that we must not depend on appearance as reported by our five senses as to what is true, and because there is poverty, sickness and misery manifested around us is no reason for us to believe such conditions either natural or necessary. They POSITIVELY are NOT NECESSARY OR NATURAL; they are extremely UNNATURAL. and those who manifest these undesirable conditions are simply doing what the woman does when she cannot cook — just ruining good material.

Everything and everybody is controlled by the same law; when we understand the law and work with it we may ask what we will and it will be done for us. Peace, happiness and prosperity are really man's natural estate.

"Consider the lilies of the field, how they grow; they toil not, neither do they spin —Wherefore if God so clothe the grass of the field — shall He not much more clothe you, O ye of little faith? Therefore take no thought (be not anxious) say, what shall we eat? or what shall we drink? or wherewithal shall we be clothed? for after all these things do the Gentiles seek —"

Let us remember that Christ was a Teacher and that He taught and demonstrated peace, power and plenty to those who believed or REALIZED the Kingdom, within. Now let us consider what He meant by "Gentiles."

Today the word means everybody who is not a Jew, but in Christ's day Gentile meant the unbeliever, the pagan, the people who worshipped idols and had no conception of the invisible God or Spirit. The Gentiles were those who looked to the outside material world and depended on the five senses altogether.

Thus we find that Christ was teaching us to depend on our indwelling spiritual power to bring forth our full supply of "whatsoever things we desire" — we must first realize our power, to do these things; second, we must sow the seed or idea by visualizing our desires mentally; third, we must have the faith to hold our ideals steadily in the face of any seeming opposition or material condition. When you can do this you will have found the "Secret Place of the Most High;" where there is no evil and no fear of evil things.

You must realize also that any inharmonious condition is apparent only. It was generated by thought and can be erased by thought. We are individualized spirit and we create our conditions with exact mathematical precision according to our character and belief. The one who has strength, faith, self-respect and love for his fellow man draws all good to himself; while the man who draws the sword of anger or criticism on his brother simply throws a boomerang for himself. The man who is healthy, happy and prosperous is the man who believes in himself, in his fellows, and the goodness of God.

Charles Hanaal in *The New Psychology*, says:

> It is in the mental realm, that last fact beyond which analysis cannot go, that all physical and

environmental effects find their common origin. In
mind is found the remedy for every ill, the solution
for every difficulty. In fact, it is the Creator's mag-
nificent provision for the emancipation of mankind.

And from every viewpoint is it not the most
intelligent, the most reasonable and the most just
arrangement that could be brought into effect for
the good of all mankind? The fact that every
human being has within himself the latent power
to realize his highest ambitions, his fondest and
noblest aspirations. Henry M. Flagler, who built
the Florida East Coast Railroad, admitted that his
success was mainly due to his ability to visualize
and hold his ideas until they became facts.

# XIV
## Health, Youth, Beauty

*Talk Health. The dreary never-ending tale*
*Of mortal maladies is worn and stale;*
*You cannot charm or interest or please*
*By harping on that minor chord, disease.*
*Say you are well, or all is well with you,*
*And God shall hear your words, and make them true.*
—WILCOX

THE HUMAN body is composed of millions of cells. These cells possess an intelligence sufficient for them to perform their individual duty in the physical anatomy. They do everything the body does: eat, drink, move, reproduce their kind, select their food, repair their waste. They also heal wounds, knit together broken bones, repel and destroy germs, etc.

Dr. Thomas J. Hudson says:

> No intelligent physician of any school claims to do more than assist nature to restore the normal conditions of the body. That it is a mental energy that is thus assisted, no one denies; for science teaches us that the whole body is made up of a confederation of intelligent entities, each of which performs its functions with an intelligence exactly adapted to the performance of its special duties.

It is a mental energy that actuates every fibre of the body. Health, like any other condition, is a matter of consciousness and is absolutely a matter of choice. Mind controls every function of the body. Take away your mind, and your body is as lifeless and as senseless as your front gate post. The central intelligence that controls each and every one of these mind organisms is the subconscious mind and as the subconscious mind accepts all suggestions and beliefs of the conscious mind as a pattern to work by, we find that our health is the product of the conscious mind.

YOUR BODY HAS NO MORE SAY-SO AS TO ITS CONDITION THAN CLAY IN THE POTTER'S HAND. JUST AS THE POTTER FORMS THE CLAY AFTER HIS OWN IDEAS, JUST SO DOES YOUR BODY CONFORM TO YOUR IDEAS AND BELIEFS. YOUR HEART, YOUR LUNGS, YOUR DIGESTIVE ORGANS MERELY CARRY OUT THE COMMANDS OF YOUR MIND. THE BODY WITH ALL ITS INTRICATE ORGANS IS THE IN-CARNATION OF IDEAS, AND THE PRESENT CONDITION OF EVERY ORGAN IN YOUR BODY IS THE RESULT OF AN IDEA.

Science has found that our bodies are constantly changing; that every eleven months we have formed an entirely new body, so far as constituent elements are concerned. Then why is it that diseased organs are constantly rebuilt in their abnormal condition when new, fresh elements are furnished them from the great storehouse of nature? It is the idea back of the organ that decides its form, and a false idea will take the pure Essence of Being and build sickness and disease.

Let us consider the control of the conscious

mind in its temporary uses. You laugh when something amusing enters your mind, you cry when something sad enters your mind, you grow pale with anger or fear, you blush with embarrassment, but always it is a thought which brings the different reactions to the body and we realize that the body is simply an instrument which the mind uses to express its emotions. It is by the same process that we impress our subconscious mind, for whatever the conscious mind accepts as true, the subconscious mind accepts as a pattern to mold our bodies by, and if you will hold before your subconscious mind the thought that weakness, disease, deformity, lameness are merely a mistake and are not real within themselves, but that the ''Image and likeness of God'' within you is perfection and the TRUTH concerning your body, you will soon be free of every ill.

You are using your creative power of thought every minute; the problem is to use it consciously and correctly, thus creating only desirable results. Cheerful, happy, constructive, loving, kindly thoughts set in motion vibrations which bring us good results. Thoughts of worry, envy, hatred, criticism and other thoughts of discord set in motion vibrations that bring bad results. Every cell in your body is intelligent and will respond to your direction and will create the exact pattern you give it. Therefore if you place a perfect ideal before the subconscious mind, its creative energies will build a perfect body. So if you wish to manifest health, your predominant mental attitude must be one of health, strength and vigor.

All the elements of nature are pure. All the forces of existence are harmonious. But man, the supreme ruler in the realm of effect, may take the perfections of Being and through his thinking processes build a world of sickness and distress. We have educated our faculties to believe inharmonious conditions real until it has become a fixed belief in the race mind that sickness, poverty and discord are necessary.

Some people believe that trials are a punishment for what we call our sins. It is true that we find many appearances of evil, but these conditions were brought about through ignorance and a belief in evil as a principle acting in opposition to good. We have not stopped to reason about this because we are so used to accepting the evidence of our senses without question.

If God is all-power, all-wisdom, and everywhere present, then where can evil be? From the viewpoint of principle, evil is not anywhere, for if God is all-power, there could not be another real power warring against Him. If that were so, He could not be all-power. If He is everywhere present (and everyone believes that God is good and God is all), then where can evil be? When we stop to analyze certain things we find ourselves obliged to give up the race thought that evil has any real power.

When we let go the idea that error of any kind

has power, we are forging toward the truth that makes men free. There is nothing to compare with the sense of freedom and joy that comes to those who realize that God is good, that good is the only reality, that good is omnipresent, and that we may draw on this limitless supply without stint or cost.

We may build strength, health, youth, and joy back into "The Temple of the Living God" that we call our body. Open your mind to the inflow of good. When you realize the fact that there is no such thing as lack, want or disease in the Universal Mind, you will see and hear and walk and laugh as you never have before. This is an individual work; each one of us must find the "Holy Grail" for himself.

Ten years ago I had a nervous collapse and upon examination it was found I was suffering from tuberculosis. The doctor put me to bed for rest and prescribed a building-up diet. Two months later I was a well woman filled with vibrant health and vitality and have never been sick a day since. I did not take any medicine. My restoration was accomplished absolutely by the power of thought. I admit frankly that for some time I did not get any visible results and there were times when I was ready to give up. This state of mind existed before I had established any basis or conscious-ness. Then one day like a flash understanding came. "ONLY WHAT I THINK CAN COME TO ME."

I had studied it and concentrated on the creative power of thought and knew it intellectually, but not until my emotional center was brought into play did I made any progress. When my subconscious mind grasped the import of my thoughts it then set about to help me.

It was not all plain sailing then, but I was fortified with the wisdom to understand why certain things happened. With understanding came the courage to go right along. I saw the light ahead and I knew I would reach it, because my arrival depended absolutely on myself. The glory of that moment will never leave me. My future depended on the use I made of my own indwelling power. I was the master of my fate, the captain of my soul. There was no real evil to beset me, and God was a just, loving Father who had placed at my disposal His boundless, limitless good, and all I had to do was to set aside all limitations, decide what I wanted, and think it into being.

I found that we must build our consciousness or faith step by step. When we make certain impressions on our subconscious mind and live for years by those impressions we cannot expect to destroy them in a few days. We must patiently substitute constructive, loving, harmonious thoughts for destructive, critical ones. The more you realize your freedom, the happier you become. Faith, joy, health, contentment, you just bubble over with these wonderful attributes and they attract the best people and environment.

I do not claim that it is easy to change our habits of thought and action, and it is harder still to disregard race thought and the evidence of the five senses, but I say emphatically that it can be done by anyone who will systematically and patiently keep on. It takes courage, determination, patience, loving kindness, and careful attention as to thought and motive. It is worth every effort for the REWARD IS SO GREAT.

Science has slowly but surely proven false all our ideas and beliefs about old age, the three score and ten length of life, the necessity of growing old and feeble. We grow old or sick or feeble for no other reason than that we believe in old age and sickness.

Everything is first an idea, and the idea of old age and sickness came about because man through ignorance trespassed the laws of his being and had to suffer the consequence of his action. Thus we find a deeply grounded belief in poverty, disease, and old age because we have had these errors given us as true all our lives. Our present conditions are the result of our demands on the Universal Life Principle. If you have traded with Life for a penny, Life will pay no more until you learn that the Universal Substance is without limit and subject to your demand.

Many years ago, Dr. Carrel, of the Rockefeller Institute, took the tissue from the heart of an embryo chicken and placed it in a culture medium. It is living and growing yet; thus demonstrating the fact that life cells will live and grow indefinitely when properly protected and nourished. Science has learned how to keep the life cells alive and grow new tissue. The problem now is how to automatically eliminate old tissue. When science learns this our lives may be prolonged indefinitely. But the secret that science is laboriously wresting from Nature, MAN HAS ALWAYS HAD THE POWER TO DO FOR HIMSELF.

Ever since Ponce de Leon made himself famous by seeking the Fountain of Youth, we have heard more or less humorous references to this supposed mythical condition; yet the only mistake Ponce de Leon made was in looking anywhere outside himself for youth. Age is a matter of condition and not years. It does not matter how many years you have lived. YOU ARE ONLY ELEVEN MONTHS OLD NOW! Your body is constantly being renewed. Every organ, every cell, every minutest part of your body, from the crown of your head to the soles of your feet, IS MADE OVER EVERY ELEVEN MONTHS. Your body cells are always building, always tearing down old tissue and building it new. Why then should you grow old, look old, or feel old? There is no reason except that you believed it necessary to grow old, because there is no principle of decay or death. "God is the God of the living and not of the dead."

It is said that if you say anything long enough and often enough folks will believe it. I may be accused of repetition in this "Key to Yourself," but I want my readers to learn the truth, and I have told it in every chapter of this book. There is no limit to your capacity of achievement. You can be what you want to be, you can do what you want to do, by the creative power of your own thought.

You are just as old as your thoughts. Every activity of your body is controlled by your mind. The saddest thing on earth is to hear men and women say: "I can't go the pace I used to. I am getting along in years." or "We are growing old now and must look ahead for old age." You can be old at thirty-five — you can be young at seventy-five. It is a matter of choice. Your mind will make you young or old according as you think youth or age.

The Universal Mind is life, health, youth, beauty, happiness, abundance in abstract perfection. Your subconscious mind is one with the Universal Mind, and you can draw on this unlimited supply for any and every thing, whatever you have believed to be true in your individual mold from which your physical condition and environment have come. Now if your physical appearance does not suit you, start right now to renewing your youth. Visualize a mental picture of physical perfection, picture every feature of your face as being perfect. To do this successfully, form an image of yourself standing beside you. If you cannot focus an image of yourself satisfactorily, select a picture or statuette that meets with your approval, one that gives you real pleasure to look at, and use it as your model. Keep it in your room; THINK of it as being you, say to yourself, "I am growing to this ideal." Never think of yourself as anything else. Learn to disregard appearance. Hold your ideal in mind as yourself and your subconscious mind will accept it as a pattern to build you by until one day you will find that it is YOU.

EVERYTHING IS THE RESULT OF THOUGHT. BEFORE ANYTHING MATERIAL CAN EXIST IT MUST BE IN THE MIND OF THE PERSON CRE—ATING IT. ALWAYS THERE MUST BE A PATTERN OR MODEL MADE OF WHAT IS DESIRED TO FORM. HERETOFORE WE HAVE MADE OUR BODIES UNCONSCIOUSLY BY HEREDITARY PATTERN AND OUR OWN SUBCONSCIOUS IMPRESSIONS. WHEN WE DO THIS BUILDING CONSCIOUSLY WE WORK BY THE SAME LAW AND OUR RESULTS ARE JUST AS CERTAIN.

It has been noticed that two peole living together have become like each other in mind and body. The keynote of Greek civilization was the love of beauty. The Greek mothers, we are told, were surrounded by models of beauty and were carefully guarded from every unpleasant sight. A bird surrounded by a certain color and seeing only that color will change its feathers to match its surroundings. Animals and birds going to a cold country where snow predominates assume white fur and plumage.

The fact that every living creature, even the tiniest forms of life, has recourse to the Universal Mind was proven by experiments at the Rockefeller Institute as follows: A rose bush infested with tiny insects was placed in a window and allowed to die. When the bush was dead, the insects, which were wingless, grew wings and flew off the bush, seeking subsistence elsewhere. These insects knew they would starve after the rose bush was dead unless they acquired the means for rapid motion, and grew wings to save their lives.

Now if the lower creatures can use the Universal Life Principle with no will except the instinctive demand for preservation of life, man with his will guided by the intelligence and knowledge of his conscious mind can do infinitely more, considering that the same law is brought into play. The same Life Principle works through both man and animal, with this difference, that whereas the lower creature works by unconscious instinctive desire, man has no restriction and can manifest anything he has the faith and knowledge to ask for. Always remember, however, that our desires must become subconscious before they come into expression, for we must BE before we can DO. THE SUPPLY IS ALWAYS EQUAL TO THE DEMAND, BUT THE DEMAND MUST BE MADE ACCORDING TO LAW AND THE LAW WORKS ONLY BY SUBCONSCIOUS DEMAND.

# XV
# Subconscious Impressions

*Leave dreaming to the fool*
*And take things as they are;*
*All things are in yourself,*
*Who stand upon a star.*

*And look upon the stars,*
*And yearn with deepening breath —*
*All things are in yourself —*
*Love and Life and Death.*

—WHEELOCK

T O ILLUSTRATE the fact that we must be before we can do, and also the fact that we do
EXACTLY WHAT WE ARE, I shall take the actual
experience of one of my friends.

He is the typical business man who started out
with a high school education and good natural
ability, plus a most charming personality. We
were discussing the phenomenal success of a
mutual friend when he said, "I would certainly
like to know his system, for I happen to know that
he has no more brains or initiative than I have and
from all appearance I have worked longer and
harder, yet everything he touches is successful,
and I am almost ready to admit that I'm a failure."

Just for an instant the courteous social mask
fell and I saw something akin to despair in his eyes
and sensed the panic of those who fight an unseen
enemy. He recovered himself quickly and tried
to change the subject, but I insisted on hearing

more and asked what the trouble was. "I don't
know," he replied, "I have ideas and work them
out, but they fail or bring profit to some one else.
I would be tiresome to go into detail but it doesn't
matter what I do or what kind of a good start I
make, I find myself right back at the beginning.
I'm forty-five years old, have no established business or position, and I believe I am getting a bit
nervous about the future."

"You are using what might be termed the Law
of Reversed Effort," I said, "same being the busy
'sidekick' of the Failure Complex: You are reaping
the results of bad subconscious impressions; let
us find out where they came from, drag them out,
and get rid of them."

After a good deal of discussion about his affairs
I learned that his first business venture had been
a failure entailing the loss of his patrimony; he
had made a new start, but subconsciously he dis-
trusted himself, perhaps because his FIRST business was a failure, and he had systematically failed,
BECAUSE SUBCONSCIOUSLY HE WAS A FAIL-
URE. Every time he failed to succeed the impression of failure grew stronger, and we find the law
working NOT in accord with his conscious efforts
but bearing the fruit of his predominant charac-
teristic. He had not understood what the trouble
was and had not made any conscious effort to
overcome the bad subconscious impression; his
health had suffered and he was rather pessimistic.

He studied psychology with me and soon
grasped the principle of success, though it was
nearly two years before he reaped real returns on

his efforts. However, he is now restored in health and is a recognized figure in business.

Another instance of the strange workings of subconscious impressions was brought to my attention by a dentist who asked me if I could figure why fate had selected him as the man whose patients ALL went to Florida. "I know it sounds absurd," he said, "but practically all my patrons have gone and I'm not doing enough business to pay office rent."

"Well," I replied, "it looks to me very much like you did not really WANT your patients." He looked his astonishment at such a finding on my part, but when I talked to him awhile I learned that while he gave satisfaction as a dentist, his heart was not in his work. His father had been a dentist and had educated his son to succeed himself. The chap in question is a mechanical genius and hates dentistry. HE HAD SUBCONSCIOUSLY DESIRED TO BE RID OF HIS WORK AND E-VENTS HAD SHAPED THEMSELVES IN AC-CORD WITH HIS INSTINCTIVE DEMAND.

Thus we find that regardless of appearance, conditions are what we subconsciously demand and the demand is based on what we inherently ARE; whether the basis be an impression acquired through our everyday experience or is hereditary, we must BE subconsciously anything we want to DO. This brings us again to the mighty power of the conscious mind because the subconscious receives its impressions from the conscious mind, and we may change any subconscious impression by systematic, determined effort. Therefore, it is absolutely necessary to control our thoughts and keep out of our minds anything that we would object to seeing brought forth in material form.

Jesus Christ gave us the truth when he said, "My words are spirit and life, they shall not return unto me void but shall accomplish that whereunto they are sent." We know that words are thought forms; you cannot think without clothing your thoughts in words. Your thoughts are a spiritual activity and spirit is life. When you learn the truth that makes men free, you will understand that your thoughts will not return to you void but will come laden with their kind, be it good or evil, constructive or destructive.

*If you don't like where you are, change what you are.*
                                              —HENRY KNIGHT MILLER

# XVI
## Desire

*When love, health, happiness and plenty hear,*
*Their names repeated over day by day,*
*They wing their way like answering fairies near,*
*Then nestle down within our homes to stay.*
—SELECTED

T HE MYSTIC ROAD to success is through the Land of Desire. After we reach the age of reason and independent action we do what we want to do. You may be inclined to argue with me about this, and say that circumstances are too strong for you, or that duty keeps you from taking a chance at gaining your desire, but any such argument simply shows a lack of understanding on your part, for the right sort of desire will break down ANYTHING that stands in the way of its fulfillment. You cannot keep a man in prison who desires hard enough to be free, and nothing can keep your own from you when you understand who and what you really are.

THE UNIVERSAL MIND IS OMNIPOTENT AND OMNIPRESENT; IT SURROUNDS YOU LIKE THE SUNSHINE AND AIR. YOUR SUB-CONSCIOUS MIND IS A PART OF THE UNIVERSAL MIND AND THROUGH YOUR SUB-CONSCIOUS SELF YOU HAVE ACCESS TO THE MIGHTY WISDOM AND POWER OF THE UNIVERSAL MIND. WHEN YOU REALIZE THIS FACT THERE IS NO LIMIT TO YOUR ACHIEVE-

MENT. FOR THE MIND DOES ITS BUILDING
SOLELY BY THE POWER OF THOUGHT. ITS
CREATIONS TAKE FORM IN EXACT ACCORD
WITH YOUR MENTAL IMAGE, AND DESIRE
BUILDS THE MENTAL IMAGE FOR YOU.

This is the secret of the power of prayer. God
is not a being to be flattered or bought by promises
into granting your desires. If that were true every
man would receive his wish for there is no one
living who has not prayed for something.

When you pray earnestly you form a mental
image of what you want, and if your faith is strong
enough you hold your desire in your thoughts;
then the Universal Mind works with you and for
you, thus bringing your desire into manifestation.
If you are lacking in material wealth or lacking in
health, it is because you do not believe or you do
not understand your own power. It is not a question of God giving you your heart's desire — EV-
ERYTHING IS OMNIPRESENT FOR EVERY-
BODY — You have only to realize your own power
and use it.

You may say that you have had a thousand
desires, you want to be rich and happy and healthy,
but you doubt, like the man who said that while
he did not believe ''all this psychology bunk,''
he'd give it a try. I suppose it is not necessary for
me to assure you that he got just what he believed,
nothing. We have so many mild desires and we do
not really believe we can obtain any one of them,
and we are so used to lightly wishing for things
that we do not KNOW WHAT WE WANT.

The Magic Secret of attainment is one INTEN-
SIVE DESIRE. Fix one goal at a time, concentrate
on just one desire. If you wanted to climb a mountain, you would not start up one path and every
little while come down and select a new trail. If
you did, you would never reach the top. It is the
same way with your desires. You have got to concentrate on one idea at a time.

Hold in mind the thing you desire most. Declare it to be an existing fact, understand that it is
YOURS, for the very moment you desire anything
it is GIVEN you, but you must hold it steady and
want it with all your heart so that the law of
growth can take effect. If you planted seed in your
garden and dug them up every little while to see if
they were sprouted or THREW THEM AWAY TO
PLANT OTHER SEED, nothing would ever grow
for you, and as the same law governs growth of
any description, you can readily see that you must
plant your thought seed and tend them with confident desire and expectation, all of which means
that you must realize that you HAVE received a
thing even before it comes forth in tangible expression.

If you can truly believe that you have received
something, your subconscious mind will surely
see that you get it. Everyone who has reaped
success has started out to accomplish just one
thing. Find out what you want, imagine things as
you want them, build new ideas of life, stop believing that some people are lucky and some must
be poor, change your ideas and find that life is a

beautiful adventure, that each day brings new opportunities to those who will lift their eyes above the everyday grind. Life means something more than animal existence. Get out of the rut, for rut is only another name for "grave." Did not the Master say, "Let the dead bury the dead, come thou and follow me." If you believe in poverty, misery and distress, you are as good as dead already.

EVERYTHING IS DONE ACCORDING TO LAW. THEREFORE, IF A PRAYER EVER HAS BEEN ANSWERED, YOURS CAN BE. IF ANYBODY HAS EVER BEEN SUCCESSFUL, YOU CAN BE. LIFE IS NOT CARRIED ON BY ANY HIT OR MISS PLAN. FOR EVERY EFFECT THERE IS COMPELLED TO BE A CERTAIN DEFINITE CAUSE. SO GET YOUR CAUSES LINED UP AND THE EFFECTS WILL TAKE CARE OF THEMSELVES.

You can have anything you want if you want it badly enough to make the proper effort to get it. Do you want health? Then study and practice the lesson on health and beauty. It matters not if you are crippled or bedridden or what the trouble is, you can have rich abounding health. Your body rebuilds itself every eleven months and you can begin any time to build a perfect body.

Is it money you want? Then realize that the soul and ideal of money is service, plant your desire for money in your subconscious mind and ask for ideas to increase your power to serve. The way for your individual success is waiting for you in the Universal Mind. Take more interest in your work and keep your mind open for new ideas; you will be guided to do the right thing at the right time. Someone has said that when we desire anything intensely, it is the thing itself trying to reach us. However that may be, the fact is that we come into understanding and right relation with our subconscious minds. THINGS JUST SEEM TO HAPPEN FOR OUR BENEFIT, and we are miraculously protected from all harm. It does not matter what calamity may happen, there is always protection for the individual.

# XVII
# Habit

*God gave all men all earth to love,*
*But since our hearts are small*
*Ordained for each one spot should prove*
*Beloved over all;*
*That, as He watched Creation's birth,*
*So we, in godlike mood,*
*May of our love create our earth*
*And see that it is good.*

—KIPLING

W E ARE creatures of habit in mind and body. Our lives, our physical conditions, our environment, show unerringly what we habitually think. Someone has said: "Sow a thought and reap an action; sow an action and reap a habit; sow a habit and reap a character; sow a character and reap a destiny."

The definition of the word "character" is: "The peculiar qualities impressed by nature or habit on a person, which separates the person possessing them from all others." Thus we find that each individual is simply the product of his or her own prevailing habits of thought and by the Law of Attraction their bodies and environment reflect what they inherently are.

We generally think of liquor, drugs, or tobacco as injurious habits and so they are, but aimless drifting, fear, worry, anger, jealousy are habits that often bring disaster more swiftly than the first mentioned three.

You cannot always prevent unpleasant things from happening, but YOU CAN DEVELOP THE HABIT OF SELF CONTROL AND WHAT HAPPENS DOES NOT MATTER BUT YOUR REACTION TO THEM IS WHAT COUNTS. The same disaster that causes one man to commit suicide will cause another to redouble his efforts and succeed. Train yourself to smile in the face of seeming defeat. The misfortunes of today are things to laugh about next year.

Every destructive emotion is a wasteful emotion. They always waste your energy and make you less able to meet a situation, whatever it may be. Great anger leaves you weak and unable to put forth your best efforts for some time, while suppressed, pent-up emotions are one of the surest causes of disease, for any destructive emotion disturbs the chemistry of your body and always causes illness in some measure.

If you find it impossible to prevent such emotions from getting started — take some sort of physical exercise while you force your thoughts into pleasant channels. Make yourself repeat an affirmation that will counteract the emotions you are trying to control. Do not try to crush all emotion from your life. Simply replace all destructive habits of thought and emotion with constructive ones. Encourage and develop your capacity to express love, happiness, contentment.

Take stock of any habit of thought and action that does not contribute to your happiness, then resolve to quit that habit right now. If you fall from grace a few times, do not waste time and energy being sorry and above all do not get discouraged, but dig right in and break the habit. Do not keep the habit on your mind, but find something of special interest to yourself and fill your days with constructive thought and action. There can be no set rule or formula for breaking undesirable habits, but the fact is that you can erase any impression on your subconscious mind, and earnest, consistent effort is your best assurance of success.

The majority of people have the poverty habit or poverty consciousness, and many other bad habits have their origin in this consciousness of lack. When a man drinks to "drown his troubles," prosperity will sometime restore his self respect and he loses the desire for liquor. Whatever the cause for any habit, I have found that to acquire the hope of freedom from material want is to gain a new attitude toward life in general. Such a mental attitude brings a new set of bright new ideas and we find ourselves on a new plane with everything changed including our habits.

# XVIII
# The Plenty Consciousness

*God meant us to be partners, you and I.*
—Selected

THE FIRST fundamental truth that you must impress on your consciousness is the fact that this Universal Mind or Energy in which you live, move and have your being is the basis of all existence.

This energy is limitless and inexhaustible. Therefore, you cannot be stinted for material to manifest anything you desire. Understand that God has never put any limit on you nor any one else. Concentrate on this one great fact until you feel yourself expanding and glowing with joy and love for everything and everybody, concentrate until you realize that the GREAT DESIRE deep in your heart is not only possible but very probable in the near future. LET THIS FACT OF BOUND-LESS PLENTY BE THE UNDEVIATING BASIS FOR ALL FUTURE THOUGHT AND ACTION.

Be patient and do not rush yourself; if you have believed in poverty and limit all your life, these traits of character are impressed on your subconscious mind and serve as a mold for your present condition. So please acquire fully a consciousness of plenty by realizing that UNFAILING SUPPLY IS THE LAW.

# XIX
# The Law of Attraction

*I hold it true that thoughts are things,*
*Endowed with being, breath and wings,*
*And that we send them forth to fill*
*The world with good results or ill.*

—EDWARDS

T HE LAW of attraction is the law of your being. It is neither good nor evil, neither moral nor immoral. It is simply a blind law that cooperates always in perfect accord with individual demand. It is the one source of perfect justice, and by its action you reap what you have sown and that which you measure unto others is measured back to you. There is no way to escape this law. You may use it consciously or unconsciously but use it you must; it is the law of Life and controls the universe with absolute undeviating precision and justice.

The benefit man receives by the operation of this law is represented by the forms of supply that add to his comfort, his human needs, and happiness AS DETERMINED BY HIM INDIVIDUALLY.

Food, clothes, money, houses, automobiles, etc., are all symbols of this law of attraction and are all related to man through this law as cause and effect, desire and response, demand and supply.

It is the operation of this law that produces such varied conditions and circumstances: riches, poverty, sickness, health, joy, sorrow. With such

a conglomeration of conditions as we see manifested on every hand, you can understand how
people came to believe in evil, poverty, disease,
and discord as being necessary somehow to human
nature. But when you realize fully that all these
conditions have no power within themselves and
are simply the results of individual thought, you
will have found the birthright of every human
being. You must first know that such a law exists
and then LIVE IN ACCORD WITH IT.

The Laws of Life and Nature do not punish or
reward man. We simply live in or out of harmony
with Nature's Laws and our happiness or misery,
health or disease, prosperity or poverty, is the
working out of the Law as cause and effect in perfect harmony with our individual demands.

This is the truth that we must understand and
live by if peace, power, love, health, happiness,
and success are to be a part of our daily life. THE
ONLY WAY TO CHANGE YOUR CONDITIONS
IN LIFE IS TO CHANGE YOUR MIND ABOUT
LIFE.

The road to happiness and prosperity begins in
one's secret thoughts, and the motive power by
which we progress along that road is constructive
emotion expressed in right action.

# XX

# Do Not Judge by Appearance

*Whatsoever we ask we receive of Him,*
*because we keep His Commandments.*
—JOHN: 3–22

LET US ASSUME that you have rid yourself of every idea of lack or limit and have established a consciousness of truth and freedom and are now ready to rebuild yourself physically and financially. You must now realize your relation to your fellow man and the fact that every human being possesses the same indwelling power that you now recognize as your greatest asset.

It is good to keep this fact in mind because it will help you to realize that any distressing condition is only a mistake and that it is in your power to help erase all such conditions by holding firmly to the fact that health, wealth, and happiness are omnipresent.

Such a realization on your part will keep you from being critical and impatient with the mistakes of your brother. If he does not understand his own power, he is a child moving in darkness and is entitled to your help. Hold all men in mind as being healthy, happy, and prosperous. When you do this you are helping others and sowing good for yourself. Always send out thoughts of love and service. They will come back to you laden with their kind.

When the Nazarene warned us not to judge and criticize each other he was simply teaching us self protection. To criticize your neighbor is to show adverse condition for yourself. "That which you measure unto others shall be measured unto you."

# XXI

# And The Greatest of These
# Is Love

*Love thyself last, and thou shall grow in spirit*
*To see, to hear, to know and understand.*
*The message of the stars, lo, thou shall hear it,*
*And all God's joys shall be at thy command.*
                                        —WILCOX

L OVE YOUR neighbor. Love yourself. When
    you retire at night and when you wake up in
the morning send a thought of love to the whole
world. When you can sincerely love everything
and everybody you will be astonished at the results, for love is the magnet that attracts the best
of everything. Love and praise your body, think
what a wonderful machine it is and how agreeably
it responds to every demand. Your body is the
mansion in which your soul and mind reside and
should be appreciated and well cared for.

# XXII
## Keying In

*Tune in to God and live.*

Y OU HAVE learned to ignore appearance; now still more important is the fact that you must guard your thoughts diligently and keep your mind on a hopeful, happy plane. KEEP YOURSELF IN A SUCCESSFUL FRAME OF MIND BECAUSE YOU RECEIVE SUBCONSCIOUSLY THOUGHTS AND IDEAS THAT CORRESPOND TO YOUR OWN STATE OF MIND. We "key in" on each other's thoughts like the radio, and receive "wireless" messages continuously.

Therefore, you can readily grasp the fact that if your thoughts are blue and discouraged, you will receive thoughts of poverty, disease, and distress; on the other hand, if your mind is clear, hopeful, and happy, you will receive the best thoughts from the best minds, and ideas thus received are sometimes very valuable.

# XXIII
## Silence is Golden

*Silence is the key that*
*unlocks the vast resources*
*of the universe.*

A NOTHER very important step toward success is to keep your affairs to yourself. Unless it is necessary to discuss your desires from a business viewpoint, do not talk of what you wish to accomplish. Concentrate on your desires, find your goal, and work towards it, but keep your own counsel. When we tell our ambitions, we waste energy and gain a certain satisfaction in hearing ourselves say what we intend to do. The man who is always telling what he is going to do never does anything.

Keep silent about every important matter. Ideas that are locked up in your secret self act as a stimulating urge and intensify your thoughts and action. If you do not talk you MUST act. Silence about your affairs gives you an inward strength and power that carries you on to success. When we want to run a mill by water power we first dam up the river.

# XXIV
## It Is Never Too Late

*Each day the world is born
anew. Each moment a new
beginning.*

R EGARDLESS of age or condition this message is written to every one. If you are middle-aged and have lost hope of ever realizing that youthful dream, read this message until your hopes are rekindled. IT IS NEVER TOO LATE. Say it over and over again. IT IS NEVER TOO LATE. MY DREAMS CAN COME TRUE. Say it until you feel new life running through you like an electric shock. Square your shoulders, breathe deep, and STEP OUT OF YOUR RUT.

If you are fifty years old, you are wise and mellowed with past experience. It will be easy for you to realize what life means. If you are seventy years old, then I say to you: "STEP OUT OF YOUR RUT, BROTHER!" You are only seventy years old because YOU THINK YOU ARE. Your body is made over every eleven months, so if you are using your birthright, you ought to be in condition to start anything you want to do. Stop telling people what you USED TO DO AND THINK WHAT YOU ARE GOING TO DO NOW. Call on the life within you, it is there — all the energy and creative power you can ever need for anything. USE IT!

I don't care what your present conditions may be, whether you are seemingly walled in by responsibilities that you cannot climb over nor crawl under, whether you are a bedridden cripple or a woman with a crowd of little children and never made a dollar in your life; the same law that brings riches and power to the captain of finance is the law that you have used to bring you poverty and disease. IT DOES NOT MATTER WHERE YOU ARE OR WHAT YOUR CONDITION IS, YOU WOULD NOT BE THERE UNLESS YOUR SUBCONSCIOUS MIND HELD THE PATTERN BY WHICH YOU LIVE.

# XXV
## More About the Subconscious Mind

*Every man's life is a fairy-
tale written by God's finger.*
—ANDERSON

YOU WILL recall that your subconscious mind is the seat of memory and habit, it is your storehouse of knowledge, and its function is to build into your life, body, and environment the result of your every thought. It also builds into your life, body, and surroundings the result of suggestions given you, and also the suggestions you have given others.

Your subconscious mind is a blind, unreasoning force and operates wholly by suggestion. It is constantly at work arranging and rearranging the details and affairs of your life to correspond with your ideas, convictions, motives, and opinions. By this method it causes the conditions in your life to become visible records of your thinking processes. If your desires are passive and not clearly defined, you become the instrument of the dominant mentalities about you. If you drift along without decision and definite purpose, you become the helpless victim of circumstance.

The way to overcome the foregoing is to set a goal of some kind; if you haven't much faith in yourself, make a resolve to accomplish something that you feel you can do by some extra effort.

THEN DO IT. Do not let anything keep you from doing what you resolve to do, for if you tell your subconscious mind you are going to do some one thing, IT IMMEDIATELY SETS VIBRATIONS IN MOTION TO GET THAT THING DONE FOR YOU, AND IF YOU DO NOT KEEP STEADY AT ONE THING UNTIL IT IS ACCOMPLISHED YOU LITERALLY THROW A MONKEY WRENCH IN YOUR MACHINERY.

Your subconscious mind is your obedient servant if you understand its power and treat it as you would a good servant, but if you do not know what you want and have no set purpose, your subconscious mind just produces a conglomeration of circumstances. Concentrate on one thing long enough and you are sure to get it. Always have a definite goal in view; never let yourself drift.

Then you must always remember that poverty, disease, and sorrow are the results of ignorance of the law of supply and while it is good to help people in any way possible we must never acknowledge any sorrowful condition as real; when we feel sympathy for people we must feel sorry for their lack of understanding rather than any adverse condition. When you find yourself being overwhelmed by any evidence of the five senses, remember that everything is made from the invisible substance all about you, that EVERY CONDITION IS AN INDIVIDUAL DEMAND BROUGHT INTO EXPRESSION BY THE LAW OF ATTRACTION, THAT EVERYTHING IS THE RESULT OF THOUGHT AND CAN BE ERASED BY THOUGHT.

# XXVI
# Disease

*Bless Jehovah, O my soul*
*Who forgiveth all thine*
*iniquities,*
*Who healeth all thy diseases.*
—PSALMS

T HE PRIMARY cause of every disease is mental
or spiritual discord, and the only permanent
basis for health and happiness is mental and spiritual harmony.

Every emotion and mental attitude creates after its kind. Intense anger with destructive intentions will attract physical injury to yourself, while fear, hate, anger, unkind criticism produce rheumatism, lumbago, headaches, stomach trouble, etc. You may gain a certain measure of relief from the foregoing by medicine, but no permanent relief is obtained until the mental discord is removed, for pain is an inharmonious mental vibration registering distress in the body cells. Anger causes high blood pressure with its kindred ills. Harsh, angry, destructive thoughts bring accident, burns, broken bones, etc. Violence is caused by violent emotions and the fear of violence.

Every phase of hate, anger, prejudice, criticism, jealousy, envy, greed, is the expression of fear in some form or other. Jealousy is the fear of losing a loved one, position, etc., and is caused by lack of self-confidence to hold your own.

111

Envy is an expression of weakness. It is the coward's snarl of defeat. The man or woman who possesses the right character never envies any one; they dig in and get their own.

Greed is a highly developed sense of want. Many men who pile up great fortunes are those who did not possess decency and comfort in childhood.

Jealousy, envy, greed, grief, cause liver and kidney trouble, constipation, biliousness. Grief, hate, and opposition cause heart trouble, hardened arteries, and congested conditions generally. Heart trouble is a specific result of mental opposition and we seldom find this disease developed except in those people who oppose the personal liberty of others. The dictator pays a fearful price for the pleasure of bending other wills to his own.

Children are the most helpless sufferers from adverse thoughts, for a child's mind is a clear, sensitive plate that receives impressions without protection. Until children are fourteen years of age their physical condition is largely the result of suggestion and impressions gathered from the adult minds about them, while the prospective mother determines to a very great extent the mental and physical conditions of her child.

# XXVII
## The Food You Eat

*A contented heart makes all
food good.*

S O FAR AS constituent elements are concerned
the human body to be properly nourished
must receive daily in the form of food, a certain
amount of proteins, fat, carbohydrates, and min-
eral salts — all of which are to be had in what we
call a balanced ration. And we know that regardless of our state of mind, we cannot be perfectly
healthy without a balanced diet. But on the other
hand, your mental state controls your appetite.
When you desire certain kinds of food it is because your mental attitude has created a demand
for the food that will make your body reflect the
state of consciousness which you possess at that
time.

You have a certain impression of yourself on
your subconscious mind, and the food you eat is
used by your body cells to sustain that subconscious image. For this reason dieting never produces the desired results.

If your subconscious image of you is too stout,
you may starve yourself and lose a few pounds,
but if you do not kill yourself, you will finally eat
what you crave and be as stout as ever. Thin people
as a rule do not eat enough of fat producing elements; if they try to eat such foods, it makes them

sick. So to change ourselves in any particular way we must go to first cause, which is mind.

It always gives us more confidence in our own ability to accomplish when we read what some one else has done. For that reason and because the following articles show such wonderful understanding, I am going to copy them verbatim.

From NAUTILUS MAGAZINE, Elizabeth Towne Co., Holyoke, Mass.:

### THINK YOURSELF THIN

*By* AGATHE R. McGIVERN

How I regained my normal weight after being 25 or 30 pounds overweight for eight or nine years.

For a long time psychology has been teaching us to think ourselves well if we are ill. For years I endured a fistula and finally had an operation for it. I was only out of the hospital a few months until it returned. I doctored almost two years trying to cure it. Finally I had another operation. This time it did not return for more than a year. When I began having that intense pain in my back again, when my legs ached so that I could not walk up and down stairs, when I became tired and listless, I knew the old trouble was there to struggle with again.

I had almost made up my mind that I would have to go to the hospital once more when I read a set of books on practical psychology. I sincerely believed in psychology. I made up my mind that I would cure myself this time. Overnight the pain in my back disappeared. Very quickly all the other symptoms followed — I was well. Now I have no pain anywhere. I have plenty of pep, I never get tired. Do not think it was easy to bring about this change. It was very hard to keep myself thinking well thoughts. To lose my doubts and fears. It was a great effort to visualize myself well.

## JUST HOW I HEALED MYSELF

I lay down several times a day, relaxed and then concentrated my thoughts on the particular spot in which I knew the trouble was. I thought how it would feel when it was well. I visualized it, and myself well. I faithfully, firmly, believed I could cure myself, that is the reason I succeeded.

I have a verse from the Bible pasted on the front of my desk which I can see as I work. 'Therefore, I say unto you, what things soever you desire, when you pray, believe that ye receive them and ye shall have them.' I think it is the easiest understood, the most encouraging verse one could remember.

## I WAS 25 OR 30 POUNDS OVERWEIGHT

Now, if I could cure myself of illness by my faith and desire alone, why could I not get thin the same way? I had been about twenty-five or thirty pounds overweight for a period of eight or nine years. I had tried desperately to reduce for I am not tall and all excess weight is very noticeable. I said I had tried to reduce. I had. I had eaten wallace bread, had gone on a vegetable diet, had starved myself, only to lose a pound or two, and immediately regained it again if I went on a normal diet. I had struggled on that way for years, never eating a bite of food, without thinking, 'This will make me fat.' I was always hungry and craved food of various kinds. I was always thinking about my meals, and the more I thought the hungrier I became. I could think of so many delectable foods, which I dared not eat because they would add to my weight. I visioned fat growing on me and how I would soon look.

After my bodily pain disappeared, one day, I thought, why not use the same principle on this fat of mine? It seemed reasonable. I tried it. Today I am normal weight. I did not starve and I did not diet nor worry about my food.

### HOW I GOT THIN

After I made up my mind, I compelled myself to think thin thoughts instead of the fat ones I had been thinking for years. I started thinking myself slender, dreamed myself slender, I ate what I wanted of any kind of food. I did not allow myself to think it would make me fat. Instead I said, over and over to myself, 'I have just eaten a normal amount, I am thinner today than I was yesterday.' I continued to think that earnestly, sincerely, I really began to get thin. Not all at once. Each week I lost a pound and gradually more.

The wonderful part about it was, and still is, I do not crave food as I did previously. When I eat, I have a satisfied feeling for a normal length of time. Taking my thoughts off of food, forgetting it except at mealtime, and then eating without a thought as to whether it will make me fat or not, has killed that terrible, longing, hungry feeling. The strange thing about it all is I do eat less than I did when I tried so hard to do without food, I am now satisfied and contented.

The secret is, my attitude of mind has changed. I now think thin thoughts.

The following is also from NAUTILUS MAGAZINE, written by G. M. E.:

One may repeat 'I am young, beautiful, healthy, happy, and prosperous' all day and receive very little return for his effort — Why? Because 'Ye shall KNOW the truth and the truth shall make you free.' Any such statement which you may repeat IS the TRUTH, and has been true for you and every one ALWAYS, but it is 'The knowledge of the truth which shall bring it to pass.'

For fifteen years after an abdominal operation I suffered intense pain in my right side. I was afraid to dance, to run, to turn over in bed, for fear the seeming lump there would give me added pain and trouble.

THEN ONE DAY I MADE A DISCOVERY WHICH SET ME THINKING. I had one intense pain elsewhere in my body, and as long as that pain lasted my right side felt as well and normal as ever it had felt. Shortly after this I took up the study of Truth and cured my side entirely because I saw it for what it was — mere fiction of my conscious mind which had become bound to me by fear. For years I had kept my mind concentrated upon that one spot, and it took a sharp pain in another part of my body attracting my attention elsewhere, to teach me the unreality of the whole thing. It was the KNOWLEDGE of the truth which set me free after years of pain and suggested operations. Concentrate upon one thing long enough and you are certain to get it — so why not concentrate upon desired conditions?

Now there is nothing too small or too great to ask of the Holy Spirit (subconscious mind, God, or what term best suits) within. I, like so many women after they hit the forty mark, had allowed myself to get too stout, with an unpleasant fullness around my waist and abdomen, with the result that nothing looked well on me. I had been doing a great deal of reading about the power of the subconscious mind, or that spark of the Divine which lives in each of us, and of how this subconscious mind is a part of Universal Mind (God). Therefore, knowing that my Father and I must be, and are one, I decided that any truth which I might decree backed by KNOWLEDGE, UNDERSTANDING AND FAITH was as the WORD OF GOD being sent out through me. Why not, therefore, speak the word which would remove this burden of superfluous fat from me?

## HOW I TREATED MYSELF
## FOR SUPERFLUOUS FLESH

Standing before the mirror, I placed my hands as I spake upon each place where I wished the 'excess baggage' removed, saying quietly but firmly,

"Attention, my Inner Being, this superfluous fat over my abdomen and hips must disappear, leaving my form slender and youthful! I rejoice and give thanks that Thou art both willing and able to do this for me."

I make this statement only when I think of it, and always look in a mirror, indicating with my hands where the fat is to be removed, for the Spirit within will do as we ask, and we must be careful to be very explicit in our demands.

Since I have started this practice, about two months ago, I measure almost four inches less around the hips and abdomen, — almost a 'perfect thirty-six ! I have done no dieting and eat whatever I wish. Speak the word, then forget about it — Let the Holy Spirit within work unhampered for "Your word shall not return unto you void, but SHALL ACCOMPLISH that where UNTO it is sent."

## WHY SHOULD I NOT, AT 42, LOOK 25?

Then there is this matter of youthfulness. I am forty-two years of age, and my friends laugh when I tell them, saying I look twenty-five. Well, why not? All the qualities God gave me are indestructible. When he conferred them on me he also gave me the wisdom and knowledge to keep them 'like new.' Not wishing to hamper me, his beloved child, he left me free to make a choice, — to keep my life, health, beauty, etc., always untarnished and indestructible, to keep my body always vitalized and renewed, to keep my beauty flawless, — or to manifest any age my conscious mind should dictate.

Of course, I might say to myself: 'Well forty-two is pretty old to look so flapperish and possess such fluffy, brown hair, I think it would be more fitting if my hair would start to turn white and a few wrinkles appear.' They will all appear if you thus insist upon them, not only in flocks, but in droves. Would that, I ask you, be showing a proper respect and love towards a kind, loving Father, who has placed in my hands and in your hands the wisdom and knowledge to attain and keep all good gifts? Practice standing before the mirror, passing your hands gently over any unsightly lines, blemishes, and say —

"All Powerful Holy Spirit within me, remove from my face every unsightly line, wrinkle and blemish, leaving it smooth and youthful. I rejoice and give thanks that Thou are both willing and able to do as I ask."

In this connection, I wish to quote from *The Lode Star* by Collier: "Every doubt, every fear, every worry that you entertain is a shackle holding Him (Holy Spirit within) back. If you can release him from all dominion of the conscious mind, (Just as I released the pain in my side from my conscious mind), if you can have the faith in Him that you would when you give a task to a trusted servant and thereafter look upon it as done, depend upon it, He will bring you what you ask for."

## THE MIND MAGNET WITHIN

The subconscious mind within each of us (Holy Spirit or God) is a vast magnet, with the power to draw from Universal Mind (God) all that we want. Don't be afraid to ask for a car, a new house, or a diamond ring. If those are the things you want — they are already yours for the asking. There is NO LIMIT to what God can give you — the only limitation is in yourself — yourself — YOUR ABILITY TO RECEIVE. When confronted with any particular desire, I say:

"I am an irresistible magnet with the power to draw unto myself everything I desire. My Father's storehouse has all abundance and there is unlimited supply (or money) available to me right now. I claim (my desire) as mine already, and that I shall very soon tangibly realize its possession. If there is anything you wish me to do, Father, give me a definite lead."

Having spoken the word, rest content. The Spirit is doing the work. Do not try to buy a car, for instance, by wondering if father, mother, or husband can be prevailed upon to give you so and so. You have no right to try and wrest from another what is rightfully theirs. If that is God's means of supplying you in that particular instance, he will open the way without any effort from you. You have just as great a share in His storehouse as father, mother or husband, and His ideas for supplying you with your share of His riches are legion. Trust Him — it pays. "Prove me now herewith, saith the Lord of Hosts, if I will not open you the windows of heaven and pour you out a blessing that there shall not be room to receive."

Do not make hard work of attaining this spiritual heritage of ours. Our Father has given us the Kingdom, only asking in return that we become as little children and "Fear not, only believe."

The first of the two foregoing articles is a practical demonstration of the fact that you must heal
yourself by your own indwelling power. We may
have operations and be assisted in many ways, but
the life within does its own healing. A doctor
must set a broken leg, but all the doctors on earth
cannot knit the broken bone together again. Only
your subconscious mind can do that for you.

I do not wish to give the impression that I
consider doctors unnecessary; this world in its
present state of consciousness would be poor indeed without the physician to ease its aches and
pains. I simply want you to recognize your own
inner self as the real healer assisted by a physician.

You will note that the lady VISUALIZED herself well, and visualized herself thin; in other
words, SHE SIMPLY GAVE HER SUBCONSCIOUS
MIND a new pattern to work by. She understood
the power of the subconscious mind and used it
correctly, although prior to her study of psychology she had used practically the same methods
that all people use who do not understand the
power they possess.

She had some sort of mental impression that
expressed itself in a fistula. She had the manifestation of that expression cut out twice but it still
persisted, showing that you cannot cut disease
out, you can only cut out the manifestation of it.
SHE CHANGED HER VIEWPOINT by studying
psychology and the disease disappeared.

When she dieted and thought of herself as fat
she was simply instructing her subconscious
mind to pile on more fat, and that is what every

one does who depends on dieting and starving to take off flesh. Follow the methods used by the lady in "Think Yourself Thin," and be as thin as you like, for your subconscious mind will faithfully reproduce your own conception of yourself.

The same rule applies to those who wish to put on flesh. Stop thinking of yourself as too thin, give your subconscious mind a perfect ideal of yourself, eat a balanced ration, and forget about it.

The second article by G. M. E. covers a wide range of mind over matter — health, youth, beauty, prosperity, happiness — I add happiness because every line she wrote expresses happiness, power and perfect understanding. If everyone who reads this little book could climb to such a state of mind, I would be happy indeed.

You will note what G. M. E. said about affirmations being of little use except when backed by knowledge; this is true, but it is by good constructive affirmation that beginners help themselves to realize truth. All forms of argument, concentration, mental images, and suggestions are simply methods by which you bring yourself to knowledge.

# XXVIII
# Your True Self

*Go not abroad; retire into thyself,*
*for truth dwells in the inner man.*
—St. Augustine

Y OUR TRUE self is the spirit of you — and the spirit of you is FOREVER COMPLETE AND PERFECT. Spirit cannot know any lack, limit or disease; IT IS THE CONSCIOUS MIND THAT PLACES LIMITS ON US IN ACCORD WITH OUR EDUCATION AND ENVIRONMENT TRAINING. There is no limit to our supply; the limitation is in our ability to receive. So we may broaden our conception of truth and enlarge our receiving powers by the use of affirmation, concentration, suggestion. You learn truth just as you would learn anything else — by study and practice.

Affirmations are a wonderful help in establishing your knowledge of your real self, for you ARE healthy, young, beautiful, prosperous, and happy, but your conscious mind must be taught to know this fact. It is not necessary to use any set form of affirmation — just make any affirmation of anything or condition that YOU WISH TO SEE MADE MANIFEST. When you can truly believe that what you say is true, nothing on earth can keep it from you provided the quality of your thought is in accord with your affirmation. By which I mean that your intentions toward all men be good and your whole attitude one of loving kindness.

# XXIX
## Prosperity

*Mental attitudes more than mental capacities cause our success or our failure.*

W HEN PAUL said: "Be anxious about nothing, but with prayer and thanksgiving make known your wants unto the Lord," he left no doubt of the fact that EVERYTHING is obtained by thought — prayer and thanksgiving — or ASK FOR WHAT YOU NEED AND GIVE THANKS THAT IT IS YOURS AT ONCE. Do not be anxious or bothered when you ask for anything; the subconscious mind sets vibration in motion to comply with your request and if you will take the shackles of doubt and fear off your Inner Self, your wishes will materialize.

The stumbling block of most people is lack of faith. The Father must do everything at once or we do not believe it can be done. And let us try to follow Paul's advice to: "Be anxious about nothing."

Just consider what such an attitude of mind would mean to you. If poverty is your chief worry, try to image how you would feel if someone gave you an income for life that would cover all your needs. You would be so happy you would want to shout for joy and you would find out that you really loved the whole world. Now is not that the way Paul meant for us to feel? And is it not a good way to start our prosperity towards us? So we are to think and act as if we had ALREADY RECEIVED.

Call on your imagination, the most wonderful power we have, and paint mental pictures of what you want. Build yourself and your environment as you would have them, build them with prayer and thanksgiving and be not anxious as to the results.

It is impossible to see two pictures at the same time; so just ignore things as they seem to be and make a perfect picture of your destiny. See yourself a perfect success, happy, healthy, and prosperous.

# XXX
# The Word of Power

*Govern the lips as they
were palace-doors, the king
within; tranquil and fair and
courteous be all words which
from that presence win.*

—ARNOLD

I N ALL ages people have believed in a Magic Word, because, wise men and prophets have spoken of the "Power of the Word." The Fable of Ben Ali and the Forty Thieves, with the magic word "Sesame," is based on this belief.

Naturally the majority of us today know that no one word could be vested with any unusual power, but what the majority do not know is that EVERY WORD YOU SPEAK IS A WORD OF POWER IN EXACT ACCORD WITH YOUR OWN CONSCIOUS POWER. Develop your knowledge of your own power and WATCH YOUR AFFIRMATIONS COME TRUE, not only for yourself but for others whom you wish to help.

"In the beginning was the word," or the beginning of everything is thought, and as every thought must be clothed in words the beginning of everything is the word. SO YOUR WORD IS THE WORD OF POWER, and whether you speak from the house tops or speak in the recesses of your own soul — your body and environment will certainly and surely reflect what you ARE.

In every line of this work I have told you the same truth. You can be healthy, happy, and successful by your own efforts and no real or lasting good can come to you except as it reflects your own state of mind.

# XXXI
## Happiness

*Happiness grows at our own firesides,
and is not to be picked in stranger's
gardens.*

—JERROLD

I F YOU would be truly happy, you must realize
that you are a spiritual being and one with God.
The Nazarene did not claim any more for Himself
than He did for all men, for He said: "He that
believeth on Me, the things that I do shall he do
also and GREATER things than these shall he do."
He understood that "I and the Father are one" and
by that understanding knew that He and all men
were EQUALLY children of God, and His message
was — "Only believe."

To be truly happy we must wipe out all fear of
God and the man-made idea of punishment. The
Prophets preached the "fear" of God, but the
word really meant respect or reverence, and we
must remember that in the past ages the masses
were ruled through fear because of their ignorance.

Another step towards happiness is to find out
the work you are best fitted to do. Many people
hate work simply because they have not found
their own place in the scheme of life.

Find out what it is that YOU LOVE TO DO,
meditate on a vocation for yourself, and when you
decide what your life work is, ask your subconscious mind to open the way for you. Go into the

Silence every day and ask until your wishes come true. Whatever you are doing — do it well — with a light heart, knowing that your present occupation is merely a stepping stone to your desires. Do not scheme nor worry, but with prayer and thanksgiving make known your wants to the Holy Spirit within.

"Go into thine inner chamber and shut the door, pray to the Father in secret, and He, hearing in secret will reward you openly."

When we consider what we do as work we are poor indeed, for whatever we do is an expression of the creative power within each individual and we should find happiness in such expression. If we do not, there is something wrong with our viewpoint in regards to work in general or we are doing something that is foreign to our indwelling talent.

Some will say that riches bring happiness; others will tell you that work brings happiness; still others will affirm that health, pleasure, love will make one happy. If that were true, all rich people would be happy, and we all know that there is less satisfaction in mere riches than any other walk of life.

If work alone brought happiness, every one who works would be happy, and so on, but we know that riches, work, health, love, pleasure, etc., do not bring happiness in themselves. True happiness is a state of mind and must come to you through recognition of your own power and the finding of your own place in the world.

# XXXII
# Thinking Is the Real Business of Life

*Thought is a magnet, and the longed*
  *pleasure,*
*Or boon, or aim, or object, is the steel,*
*And its attainment hangs but on the measure*
*Of what thy soul can feel.*

—WILCOX

A S REGARDS life in general and our relation to the material needs of man we have placed our cart before the horse in this wise. Looking on our conscious needs we figure from the viewpoint of the five senses and literally dig our bread by the sweat of our brow, never CONSIDERING THE INDWELLING SPIRITUAL WEALTH, AND NINE-TENTHS OF US NOT KNOWING THE SPIRIT IS WEALTH.

It is tragic to see people striving and struggling for existence when the good things of life are yours for the asking. Not only yours to ask for, but YOURS BY DIVINE RIGHT! God is spirit, you are spirit, and every manifested thing is made from the spiritual energy that is all around us. Therefore, the proper way to acquire anything is to ask your subconscious mind for it. You are God's child just as surely as you are the child of your human father and He is just as interested in your welfare and just as anxious to give you your desires as the very kindest and most loving material father, with the following advantage from the spiritual viewpoint.

Whereas, your earthly father can withhold his blessing through caprice of any kind, God has established the Law of Attraction so that each and every one of us may be given strict justice. You cannot acquire and HOLD anything that is not in accord with your predominant mental attitude, neither can you be robbed of anything that is yours by subconscious right. When right-thinking people seem to lose something, it is their Inner Self clearing the way for better things.

When you ask for anything in spirit, you are complying with the Law and ALLOWING the Law to work through you unhampered by the doubts, fears, and restrictions of the conscious mind. When you fail to recognize your spiritual wealth, you cut yourself off from your source of supply and your subconscious self is powerless to do anything except to LET YOU WORK JUST AS HARD AS YOU THINK IT NECESSARY.

# XXXIII
## The Unseen Pattern

*No mortal yet has measured his*
*    full force.*
*His, a river rising in God's thought*
*And emptying in the soul of man.*
                        —WILCOX

S OIL, WATER, sunshine, and air contain every
    element necessary to sustain life on every
plane of consciousness.

In the vegetable kingdom we find thousands
of different kinds of trees, shrubs, and flowers;
each specie draws its own portion to sustain life
and growth, but its color and form are decided by
Nature's secret pattern.

In the animal kingdom we may take a kitten
and a puppy — feed them exactly the same food,
house and care for them the same way, but each
of them will develop the color, form and characteristics of its own breed because, regardless of
every material condition the unseen pattern of
each must be followed.

Coming to man, we may give identically the
same food and attention to babies, each represent-
ing a different human race type, and the race consciousness of each individual type will furnish the
pattern for its growth, color, and character, in
utter disregard of external conditions. The pattern
or mold for each one exists on the unseen side of
life, and must express in exact accord with its own
consciousness. THAT IS THE LAW.

We are bound by our own consciousness but man, above all living creatures, has the power to build himself individually by working with the law to CREATE AND EXPRESS HIS VERY OWN UNSEEN PATTERN. Concentrate on the foregoing until you understand it thoroughly. THE UNSEEN IS THE WORLD OF CAUSE. That which we see manifested has no power within itself; it is simply the result of unseen pattern.

You have come to understand that there is no lack of the basic material from which all things are made. You may lack this or that thing in materialized form, but there cannot be a lack of Universal Substance, though this substance or energy can only manifest for you in exact accord with your own unseen pattern, or if you just drift along with no definite desire, then the RACE CONSCIOUSNESS STEPS IN and hands you the things that are usual for people of your age and hereditary development.

# XXXIV
# Caution

*The earth is yours and mine*
*Our God's bequest.*
*That testament divine*
*Who dares contest?*
                                    —WILCOX

Y OUR MIND and its present state of development controls the materialization of the Universal Mind through you. Your present subconscious impressions determine exactly what you
are now. So please do not jump to the conclusion
that you can read the truth set forth herein and go
right out and start manifesting an entirely new
set of conditions.

An acorn is the seed of a mighty oak, but the
law of growth must unfold and build up the tree.
And while the Holy Spirit within you is not subject to time in the same way that a tree must be,
you must gain understanding through meditation
and study, for a new consciousness must be developed before a new set of conditions can arise.

A person who has thought in limited terms
cannot, at first, picture himself possessing and
using a huge amount of money; but he can see
himself spending wisely a reasonable amount and
can gradually entertain the idea of a million dol-
lars. To keep your equilibrium, your consciousness must change first, causing new ideas, which
in turn makes new and larger demands on your
subconscious mind. These demands will be met
in perfect accord with the unseen pattern or mental picture held by you.

# XXXV
# Time

*It may make a difference*
*to all eternity whether we*
*do right or wrong today.*
—CLARKE

TIME is not a prime factor in the building of our consciousness. One person may be able to get results quickly, while others will be months reaching any satisfaction, while some will be years learning the truth. You may learn more in ten minutes of intense concentration than you would in a month's ordinary thinking.

Your progress depends on your ability to eject old ideas and set opinions. You are fortunate if you have no set opinions, for every generation brings a new set of scientific facts to set aside what everyone thought was the acme of wisdom. There can be no progress without change. So keep an open mind. Do not declare anything false just because you do not understand it. Dig in and find out what it is all about. Be up to date in worthwhile things and take a friendly interest in everything about you.

# XXXVI
## Depend on Yourself

*This much I know*
*That Thou art always near*
*Beyond all sky and farthest Space.*
*Thou art unmeasured lone,*
*Miraculous to fill, Eternal vastness*
*And my inmost heart.*

—MOON

T HE HARDEST work you have to do is to learn to depend on your Inner Self because you have been taught to look always to someone else.

As small children we depended on mother; later we looked to both parents for everything. When we take our place in the world as a wage earner the job is of paramount importance. The married woman sees no means of support except her husband. Always we have looked outside of ourselves.

It is perfectly right and proper that small children should depend on their parents, but they should be taught to recognize their own power and to use it. Every man should work but should not depend on the job as his only means of support. Such a mental attitude makes one afraid, and fear causes tenseness and strain.

On the other hand, the man who knows that his material wealth really depends on his state of mind will do better work, be healthy, happy, and if he loses a job, instead of being upset, will simply recognize an opportunity to better his condition — for when changes begin to occur, one of two things is going to happen, you are either going to land in a better position or you are going backward, and whatever occurs will be in strict accord with your predominant state of mind. In any event, when you cannot see your way clearly DO NOT GET BLUE, but calmly, steadily hold a mental picture of what you want. If you are seeking a position, keep yourself in a hopeful frame of mind and depend on your subconscious mind to guide you to do the right thing, for oftentimes what we want is hidden behind something else. Therefore, if a position is open for you, take it with the mental reservation that it is a stepping stone to what you want.

Do not ever let your mind lean on anything or on any person; your good or support may come through the obvious channel, but the Universal Mind can create any number of ways and means for you IF YOU BUT RECOGNIZE THIS TRUTH and live by it. A word to the wives and mothers who do not earn any money. Yours is the most important position on earth; you wield the mightiest power, and your responsibility is the greatest, for nine times out of ten, your child will not depart from your training. Your mental outlook and your spiritual strength is of paramount importance, yet I find the wife and mother the most difficult pupil, because of her idea of dependence on her husband.

Now let us go back to the First Cause; the Universal Mind (God) is the spirit, life, mind of every individual — the same life that operates through your husband is your life; the same mind that manifests through him finds expression through you. You are both individualized spirits, and your latent powers of expression are equal.

In the cooperative necessity of family life, your husband provides and you bear children and make a home, BUT IN THE EYES OF GOD YOU ARE SIMPLY TWO OF HIS CHILDREN WITH ABSOLUTELY EQUAL RIGHTS IN YOUR DE-MANDS ON HIS INFINITE ABUNDANCE.

There is nothing wrong with a man supporting his family, it is his blessed privilege to do so; I just want the wife to understand that she has the same power to gain her desires through recognition of her subconscious mind as her husband and that her mental pictures are just as sure to materialize as those of a captain of finance.

The means to gain your desires may come through your husband or you may be given ways and means through other channels — the important thing for you to know is that, because you are busy bearing and rearing children is no reason for you to believe that you cannot be as independent mentally as the woman who receives a pay envelope. Consider your husband as a beloved partner in the business of homemaking AND LOOK TO GOD AS THE UNFAILING SOURCE OF SUPPLY FOR YOU BOTH.

To the husband I say: God is your silent partner, the one and only source of all you have or will ever acquire. Do not carry all the burden, give your Father a chance to materialize through you what you desire for the good of yourself and loved ones. Realize the all-embracing Life Substance about you and recognize the Law of Attraction as your most efficient aid. God is not only willing, but eager to express in external conditions anything you give him a pattern for. ALWAYS REMEMBER IT IS THE SEED YOU SOW THAT DECIDES THE NATURE OF YOUR PRODUCT.

If you are already a student of psychology, you will know that the facts set forth herein are true. If you are a beginner, you may be a bit confused as to the meaning conveyed, thus it behooves you to take each chapter and study it carefully.

Every time you read a sentence you will gather a better understanding; something you have passed over before will attract your attention and by degrees a new world of infinite beauty and achievement will open before you.

When you have reached a reasonable degree of understanding, make your own affirmation to suit your own needs and apply the truth after your own ideas — develop your own inner power — and use it for your every need and desire. Read some part of this book every day, read. it through at least once a week. Concentrate with undivided attention half an hour every day, and keep an affirmation handy to repeat when you think of it or when the need arises.

In this way you will reach your goal; and whether it be money, power, love, health, happiness, social or political position—whether you choose one or choose all—the fulfillment lies in the Universal Mind awaiting your realization to make your dreams come true.

## SALUTATION TO THE DAWN

Look to this day, for it is Life,
The very Life of Life.
Within its brief span, lie all the Verities,
And realities of your existence.
The Bliss of Growth.
The Glory of Action.
The Splendor of Beauty.
For yesterday is but a Dream
And tomorrow is but a Vision
But today well lived makes every
Yesterday a dream of happiness
And every tomorrow a vision of Hope.
Look well therefore to this day.

—THE SANSKRIT


THE END

# A BRIEF BIOGRAPHY

Although the book, KEY TO YOURSELF, was no doubt the greatest single accomplishment of her career, Dr. Venice J. Bloodworth was also known through her works, to many people within and around the vicinity of Atlanta, Georgia, as teacher, counselor, and friend.

Venice Bloodworth received her doctorate in psychology from Northwestern University, Chicago. The content of her teaching, and the practice of her chosen profession reflect both the findings of modern psychologists, and the principles taught hundreds of years ago by Jesus of Nazareth. In describing her work she has said this: "The method is always the same, regardless of what is to be accomplished. First, the idea. Second, visualizing the idea. Third, manifesting the idea. First we make a decision; then, we use the marvelous function of the mind, the imagination, which I call the workshop of the mind, to visualize this change. Since it is a law that energy follows thought, then when the thoughts are flowing in a positive manner, we get positive results."

She shared her formula for health, beauty, joy, harmony, and richer living through several avenues: writing, private consultations, public lectures, and class work. Dr. Bloodworth referred to her subject matter as Spiritual Psychology, and set for her purpose in teaching the goal of helping humanity, by explaining to people that they can THINK themselves into actually being well, happy, prosperous, and beautiful. In addition she provided helpful suggestions as to how her students might nurture this belief, and thus stay with it, until the desired changes appeared either in form or experience.

The personal affirmation she used to begin her day's activities was this: "I am whole, perfect, strong, powerful, loving, harmonious, and happy." Standing before her mirror, she repeated these words for about ten minutes each day. Evidence of the effectiveness of her belief came to her in many ways. For instance, she discarded her glasses after realizing that her eyes were "whole and perfect, and continually rebuild themselves."

When Dr. Bloodworth was around thirty years of age, she decided that this was "such a nice age to be" that she resolved to retain her youthful appearance, by remaining as she was then. This she did most successfully. In fact, when she was beyond fifty she was continually taken for a woman as young as the age she had named for herself.

Upon three different occasions this petite, lovely, and gracious lady was offered roles in motion pictures, which she did not accept. She preferred to help the sick and frustrated regain health and happiness, and those who had lost their way to become rehabilitated and useful citizens.

Her interests extended to many areas of helpfulness, including lectures to PTA groups on child psychology, and work with the Atlanta Council of Church Women at the Atlanta Prison Farm, and the Georgia Training School for Girls. KEY TO YOURSELF was written over a period of several years, along with the demands of her professional practice, which she carried on in her farm home near Kenesaw Mountain.

Although Dr. Venice Bloodworth was devoted to the service of humanity, she found time also for a normal, well-balanced personal life. As a homemaker and wife, she spent many happy years with her husband, James A. Bloodworth, a railroad official. Together they enjoyed the comfort of their farm home, along with the collection of animals they took with them back into their wooded mountain retreat. There was Mike, the dog, a mare named Honey, and a pair of cats called Ike and Mamie. The cat family grew, as cat familes will, to include three kittens: Napoleon, the proud one, Rastus Densenberry, who was by nature "sort of slow," and Loving Sam, whose name was well suited to his personality.

In acknowledgment of help received, the Bloodworth home was richly showered by tokens of gratitude from patrons, from many points around the world. Their library too was representative of many interests, containing a wide variety of reading matter, from the purely inspirational to mystery novel; books to inform, to live by, and for entertainment and relaxation.

The tenor of Dr. Bloodworth's life was a harmonious reflection of the philosophy she taught.

# IN MEMORIAM

On January 17, 1956, Venice Bloodworth embarked on another journey; one which took her beyond the frontiers of human experience into an unfamiliar realm of spiritual unfoldment. Those who knew her personally, or have found strength, courage, and inspiration in her work realize how well she must have known her way. The joy of her belief, or the peace of her understanding surely cannot be lost to her, even as they have not gone from those who have been blessed by them.

To her many friends and pupils Venice Bloodworth left a rich legacy; one that emerged through the love that impelled her to record her innermost thoughts, and the conviction of her heart. It is a legacy which enriches you first by the attention given to her written words. Its value is enhanced as the ideas gleaned are employed in daily living. In due time it is wondrously expanded as you share your legacy through the radiance of Truth and Beauty which expresses within and around you.

Memory lives, then, not as a person departed, but as the achievements of a lifetime that continue to fill an ever widening Circle of Love.